Ibrahim Uddin

CW01667896

New Revised Edition

تسهيل الصرف

EASY ETYMOLOGY

ZAM ZAM PUBLISHERS

ZAM ZAM

Publishers, Book Sellers & Exporter

Fifth Authorized Edition 2015

Title : **Easy Etymology**

1st Published : October 2006

Pages : 108

Published By:

Zam Zam Publishers

Urdu Bazar Karachi-Pakistan.
Ph : 0092-21-32760374
0092-21-32729089
Fax : 0092-21-32725673
E-mail : zamzampublisher@gmail.com

Visit Our Website

www.zamzam Publishers.com

Books Also Available in :

AZHAR ACADEMY LTD.
54-68 Little liford lane
Manor Park London E12 5QA
Phone: 020-8911-9797

MADRASAH ARABIA ISLAMIA
1 Azaad Avenue P.O Box 9786,
Azaadville 1750 South Africa
Tel: 00(27)114132786

USMANI BOOK CENTRE
129 the Broadway, Perry Barr,
Birmingham B20 3ED
Phone: (0) 121 344 4165

GANGAT`S
Lusaka Zambia
P.O Box# 33319
Tel: +260-95-88-0990

AL FAROOQ INTERNATIONAL
68 Asfordby Street Leicester
LE5-3QG
Tel: 0044-116-2537640

ISLAMIC BOOK CENTRE
119-121 Halliwel Road,
Bolton BI 1 3NE U.K
Tel/Fax: 01204-389080

DARUL ULOOM AL MADANIA
182, Sobieskist, Buffalo,
NY. 14212 U.S.A

ZEENAT EMPORIUM
6348 N.Campbell Ave, Chicago
Tel: 773-274-8055 & 773-430-8055
Fax: 847-6792285

FOREWORD

باسمه تعالى

نحمده ونصلي علي رسوله الكريم

Almighty Allah chose the Arabic language to deliver His final message to humanity. This fact, in itself tells of the comprehensiveness, splendor and beauty of the language. As an Arabic adage runs:

كَلَامُ الْمُلُوْكِ مُلُوْكُ الْكَلَامِ

The speech of kings is the king of speech.

Consider, also the fact that Arabic was an inherent Sunnah of the Messenger of Allah, Muhammad ﷺ. Hence, there can be no doubt that any attempt to propagate this language or facilitate others in learning it is praiseworthy and indeed a means of attaining great rewards in the Hereafter.

Arabic grammar is made up of mainly two branches, i.e. Nahw (syntax) and Sarf (etymology and morphology). Numerous books are available in English on the former subject. However, to the knowledge of the writer of these lines, a formal textbook in the English language, exclusively pertaining to the latter subject, elaborate, replete with examples and exercises and written in a style which the Darul Uloom usually prefer, is not available.

Thus, it is immensely pleasing to see a book on this subject finally appearing in our midst. May Allah create greater enthusiasm in our fellow Muslims to serve Islam according to their own capacities and capabilities.

I have read this book from cover to cover and, along the way have also offered some suggestions. I am certain that this book will be appreciated by all Darul Uloom students and will thus alleviate many of the problems they encounter in this field.

May Allah accept this work and make it a means of salvation for the ummat at large. Ameen.

Ml. Hassen Dockrat (Lecturer and Author)
12 Rajab 1421

PREFACE

Easy Etymology is a simplified, concise, grammar textbook aimed at beginners in the study of the Arabic language. A special feature of this work is that each chapter has been divided into 5 sections. viz. Vocabulary, Definitions, Paradigms, Laws and Exercises. This facilitates easy learning for students. Between two and five new words are introduced in each new lesson and these words recur throughout the text. It is expected that the pupil will assimilate over a hundred basic Arabic verbs as well as their multiple varied forms.

Laws are introduced gradually and a step-by-step explanation is provided for their correct usage. The oral drill method is required to attain proficiency and fluency in the paradigms. The variety of exercises develops the ability to practically apply etymological laws.

The following textbooks were referred to in compiling this work, viz.
'Ilmus Sarf' by Moulana Mushtaaq Ahmed Saheb Cherthawali {رحمه الله تعالى}
'Kitaabus'Sarf' by Hafiz Abdur Rahman Saheb Amrattasri {رحمه الله تعالى}
'Towdeehun Nahw' by Moulana Hassen Dockrat { دامت بركاتهم }
'Arabi ka Muallim' by Moulana Abdus Satar Khan {رحمه الله تعالى}
and 'A new Arabic Grammar' by Haywood and Nahmad.

The author asks the reader's forbearance for any shortcomings in this modest attempt and welcomes any suggestions for further improvements to the textbook.

Rabi-ul-Awwal 1424
May 2003

ACKNOWLEDGEMENTS

Firstly, I thank Allah Subhaanahu Wa Ta aala for His infinite bounties.
Then, a sincere thanks is forwarded to Moulana Hassen Dockrat (Author of A simplified Arabic Grammar and lecturer at the Daarul Uloom) for patiently and painstakingly scrutinizing and correcting this text and also for writing the foreword.

A heartfelt vote of thanks goes to Aalima Kadwa for typing the English and Aalima Gundiwalla for typing the Arabic as well as presenting the book in its final form.

Many thanks are extended to the institute that has undertaken the publication of this book.

I am also greatly indebted to my teachers and last but not least to my spouse who was a great source of encouragement and assistance to me.

May Allah accept this humble effort.

Hoosein Loonat
0721084441
0114131071
South Afirca
munawwar.azaad@gmail.com

TABLE OF CONTENTS

LESSON 1
PAST PERFECT ACTIVE POSITIVE VERB

اَلْبَحْثُ : اَلْفِعْلُ الْمَاضِيْ اَلْمَعْرُوْفُ اَلْمُثْبِتْ

A : Vocabulary:

ضَرَبَ
He hit.

B : Definitions:

1.) Sarf is the study of that branch of Arabic grammar which deals with the formation, recognition and changing of words from one form to another. It also deals with the correct sequence of the Arabic conjugation (gardaan).
Benefit: It enables one to read and translate words correctly.
Object: To ultimately understand the Qur aan Al Majeed and Ahadeeth Al Mubarakah thereby gaining the pleasure of Allah Ta aala.

2.) اَلْبَحْث - Subject under discussion.
3.) اَلْمُثْبِتْ / اَلاِثْبَات - Positive. i.e. for an action to occur e.g. I ate as opposed to I did NOT eat.
4.) اَلْفِعْلُ الْمَاضِيْ - Past tense verb e.g. The boy kicked the ball (in the past).
5.) اَلْمَعْرُوْف - Active, where the doer is known e.g. Zaid hit Amr. One is aware of who perpetrated the action of hitting.
6.) صيغة - (Mood/form) A form or forms of a verb indicating fact, command, tense, number, etc.
7.) گردان - (Paradigm/ conjugation / inflection) An Urdu term indicating the process or practice of rendering the various forms of the word in its correct order.

C : Conjugation:

He (1 man) did	وَاحِدْ مُذَكَّرْ غَائِبْ	فَعَلَ
They (2 men) did	تَثْنِيَهْ مُذَكَّرْ غَائِبْ	فَعَلَا
They (all /many men) did	جَمْع مُذَكَّرْ غَائِبْ	فَعَلُوْا
She (1 woman) did	وَاحِدْ مُؤَنَّثْ غَائِبْ	فَعَلَتْ
They (2 women) did	تَثْنِيَهْ مُؤَنَّثْ غَائِبْ	فَعَلَتَا
They (all /many women) did	جَمْع مُؤَنَّثْ غَائِبْ	فَعَلْنَ
You (1 man) did	وَاحِدْ مُذَكَّرْ حَاضِرْ	فَعَلْتَ
You (2 men) did	تَثْنِيَهْ مُذَكَّرْ حَاضِرْ	فَعَلْتُمَا
You (all / many men) did	جَمْع مُذَكَّرْ حَاضِرْ	فَعَلْتُمْ
You (1 woman) did	وَاحِدْ مُؤَنَّثْ حَاضِرْ	فَعَلْتِ

You (2 women) did	تَثْنِيَة مُؤَنَّث حَاضِر	فَعَلْتُمَا
You (all / many women) did	جَمْع مُؤَنَّث حَاضِر	فَعَلْتُنَّ
I (1 man / woman) did	وَاحِد مُذَكَّر و مُؤَنَّث مُتَكَلِّم	فَعَلْتُ
We (all / men / women) did	تَثْنِيَة وجَمْع ،مُذَكَّروَمُؤَنَّث مُتَكَلِّم	فَعَلْنَا

In Arabic every verb has fourteen forms with each form incorporating the following:
1.) Number, (i.e. singular, dual or plural)
2.) Gender, (i.e. masculine or feminine)
3.) Person, (i.e. first person, second person or third person.)
4.) Tense, (either past, present or future)
5.) Positive or negative,
6.) Active or passive.

The above conjugation / گردان is of the basic Arabic verb- فَعَلَ which means, He (one man) did.
It incorporates all the factors mentioned above.
The first three factors make up the segha i.e. it describes the form or mood of the verb. Thus the verb فَعَلَ is firstly - singular, secondly masculine and thirdly, in the third person. The segha will thus be وَاحِد مُذَكَّرْ غَائِبْ i.e Singular Masculine Third person.

The last three factors make up the بَحْث i.e. the TOPIC under discussion. Hence, the basic Arabic verb فَعَلَ is firstly a positive verb i.e. he did an action contrary to he did not do an action.
Secondly, it is a past tense verb i.e. he did the action in the past and not now in the present.
Thirdly, it is an active verb. In this verb the doer is known. Thus in "He did" the doer is "He" and he is the person actively involved in the action. He is doing the work. The work is not being done upon him. He is not a passive participant in the action.
e.g. قَتَلَ زَيْدٌ Zaid Killed

We are aware that Zaid committed the action of killing. Zaid is thus the doer.

The بحث (topic) of the فَعَلَ gardaan will be اَلْبَحْث اَلْفِعْلُ الْمَاضِيْ الْمَعْرُوْف الْمُثْبِت
The letters at the end of the words are known as عَلَامَاتُ الْمَاضِي i.e. the signs of مَاضِيْ
There are thus fourteen signs of الْمَاضِيْ :

تَ	نَ	اتَا	اتْ	وا	ا	ـَ
نَا	تُ	تُنَّ	تُمَا	تِ	تُمْ	تُمَا

Note: The occurrence of any of the above DOES NOT ALWAYS mean that the word is a اَلْفِعْلُ الْمَاضِي
e.g. مُسْلِمُوْنَ يَفْعَلْنَ

D: Exercises:

1.) Draw up the conjugation tables of:

a.) ضَرَبَ b.) كَتَبَ He wrote c.) إِجْتَنَبَ He refrained d.) اَكْرَمَ He honoured

2.) Translate:

a.) ضَرَبْنَا b.) كَتَبْتُمْ

c.) فَعَلْتُنَّ d.) اِجْتَنَبَتْ

e.) ضَرَبْتُ f.) كَتَبْنَ

3.) Translate:

a.) We hit. b.) You (1 woman) wrote.

c.) She refrained. d.) I hit.

4.) Define:

a.) اَلْاِثْبَات b.) اَلْفِعْلُ الْمَاضِي c.) اَلْمَعْرُوْف d.) صِيغَه E.) گردان

5.) Identify all the اَلْأَفْعَالُ الْمَاضِيْ **in the following ayaat:**

١) ﴿فَإِنْ اَعْرَضُوْا فَمَا أَرْسَلْنٰكَ عَلَيْهِمْ حَفِيْظًا اِنْ عَلَيْكَ اِلَّا الْبَلٰغُ وَاِنَّا اِذَا اَذَقْنَا الْاِنْسَانَ مِنَّا رَحْمَةً فَرِحَ بِهَا وَاِنْ تُصِبْهُمْ سَيِّئَةٌ بِمَا قَدَّمَتْ اَيْدِيْهِمْ فَاِنَّ الْاِنْسَانَ كَفُوْرٌ﴾ (سورة الشورى: ٤٨)

٢) ﴿وَلَمَّا فَتَحُوْا مَتَاعَهُمْ وَجَدُوْا بِضَاعَتَهُمْ رُدَّتْ اِلَيْهِمْ قَالُوْا يَا اَبَانَا مَانَبْغِيْ﴾ (سورة يوسف: ٦٥)

٣) ﴿قَتَلَ دَاوٗدُ جَالُوْتَ﴾ (سورة البقرة: ٢٥١)

6.) Identify all the past tense verbs in the following sentences:

١) وَجَاءَ يَوْمُ عِيْدٍ فَفَرِحَ النَّاسُ.

٢) وَخَرَجَ النَّاسُ وَخَرَجَ الْأَطْفَالُ.

٣) وَذَهَبَ النَّاسُ وَبَقِيَ إِبْرَاهِيْمُ فِي الْبَيْتِ .

٤) وَغَضِبَ الْإِخْوَةُ جِدًّا لَمَّا سَمِعُوْا الرُّؤْيَا وَاشْتَدَّ حَسَدُهُمْ .

٥) فَنَقُوْلُ لَهُ: صَدَقْتَ يَا اَبَانَا قَدْ أَكَلَهُ الذِّئْبُ.

٦) وَرَجَعَ الْإِخْوَةُ إِلَى الْبَيْتِ وَتَرَكُوْا يُوْسُفَ فِي الْبِئْرِ .

٧) أَكَلَ الْإِخْوَةُ الطَّعَامَ وَنَامُوْا عَلَى الْفِرَاشِ .

٨) وَعَطِشُوْا فِي الطَّرِيْقِ وَبَحَثُوْا عَنْ بِئْرٍ .

٩) وَدَخَلَ يُوْسُفُ فِي السِّجْنِ وَعَرَفَ أَهْلُ السِّجْنِ جَمِيْعًا أَنَّ يُوْسُفَ شَابٌّ كَرِيْمٌ .

١٠) وَسَأَلَ الْمَلِكُ عَنْ يُوْسُفَ وَعَلِمَ الْمَلِكُ أَنَّ يُوْسُفَ بَرِيءٌ .

LESSON 2
VERB FORMS

اَلصِّيْغَة

A : Vocabulary:

سَمِعَ
He heard.

B : Definitions:

1.) اَلصِّيْغَة -(mood or form) the explanation of a verb or noun, i.e. a form or forms of a verb indicating fact, tense, command, number etc.

2.) وَاحِدْ -singular e.g. one boy

3.) تَثْنِيَة - dual e.g. two boys

4.) جَمَعْ - plural e.g. 3 boys, 8 boys

5.) مُذَكَّرْ - masculine

6.) مُؤَنَّثْ - feminine

7.) غَائِبْ - the third person i.e. a person who is absent e.g. فَعَلَ "He did."

8.) حَاضِرْ - addressee or the second person. i.e. A person is present. The person who is being spoken to and is referred to as "you" e.g. فَعَلْتَ "You did."

9.) مُتَكَلِّمْ - the speaker who is generally referred to as the first person. It is used when talking of oneself. e.g. فَعَلْتُ "I did.", فَعَلْنَا "We did."

C:

The word فَعَلَ refers to a single absent male who is the doer of the action. The translation will thus be, "He one man did". The اَلصِّيْغَة (form) will be: singular masculine third person. i.e. وَاحِدْ مُذَكَّرْ غَائِب

Refer to lesson 1 C

D: Exercises:

1.) Write out the اَلصِّيْغَة (form) and بحث (subject) of the following:

A.) سَمِعْنَا	b.) ضَرَبْتُنَّ	c.) كَتَبْتُمْ	d.) اِجْتَنَبَ	e.) فَتَحَتْ
f.) كَرُمَا	g.) حَسِبْنَ	h.) نَصَرْتَ	i.) دَخَلْتِ	j.) جَعَلْتُمَا

2.) Translate and write the Arabic of the following seghas using the word سَمِعَ.

a.) وَاحِدْ مُذَكَّرْ حَاضِرْ b.) جَمْعْ مُؤَنَّثْ غَائِبْ c.) تَثْنِيَهْ مُذَكَّرْ حَاضِرْ

d.) وَاحِدْ مُؤَنَّثْ حَاضِرْ e.) جَمْعْ مُذَكَّرْ وَمُؤَنَّثْ مُتَكَلِّمْ f.) تَثْنِيَهْ مُذَكَّرْ غَائِبْ

g.) وَاحِدْ مُذَكَّرْ و مُؤَنَّثْ مُتَكَلِّمْ h.) جَمْعْ مُذَكَّرْ غَائِبْ i.) وَاحِدْ مُؤَنَّثْ غَائِبْ

j.) جَمْعْ مُؤَنَّثْ حَاضِرْ k.) تَثْنِيَهْ مُؤَنَّثْ غَائِبْ l.) وَاحِدْ مُذَكَّرْ غَائِبْ

3.) Define:

a.) اَلصِّيْغَة b.) وَاحِدْ c.) مُذَكَّرْ d.) جَمْعْ e.) غَائِبْ

f.) مُؤَنَّثْ g.) مُتَكَلِّمْ h.) حَاضِرْ i.) تَثْنِيَة

4.) Draw up the conjugation table of: سَمِعَ

5.) Identify all the past tense verbs in the following ayaat and also write down the seghas (forms) thereof:

١) ﴿لَقَدْ كَفَرَ الَّذِيْنَ قَالُوْا﴾ (سورة المائدة: ١٧)

٢) ﴿قَدْ خَلَتْ مِنْ قَبْلِهِ الرُّسُلُ وَأُمُّهُ صِدِّيْقَةٌ كَانَا يَأْكُلَانِ﴾ (سورة المائدة: ٧٥)

٣) ﴿ذٰلِكَ كَفَّارَةُ أَيْمَانِكُمْ إِذَا حَلَفْتُمْ﴾ (سورة المائدة: ٨٩)

٤) ﴿فَلَمَّا نَسُوْا مَا ذُكِّرُوْا بِهِ فَتَحْنَا عَلَيْهِمْ﴾ (سورة الانعام: ٤٤)

٥) ﴿حَتّٰى إِذَا فَرِحُوْا بِمَا أُوْتُوْا أَخَذْنَاهُمْ﴾ (سورة الانعام: ٤٤)

٦) ﴿قَالَ أَرَأَيْتَ إِذْ أَوَيْنَا إِلَى الصَّخْرَةِ فَإِنِّيْ نَسِيْتُ الْحُوْتَ﴾ (سورة الكهف: ٦٣)

٧) ﴿نَسِيَا حُوْتَهُمَا فَاتَّخَذَ سَبِيْلَهُ﴾ (سورة الكهف: ٦١)

LESSON 3
PAST PERFECT NEGATIVE ACTIVE VERB

اَلْبَحْث نَفِي الفِعْلُ الْمَاضِيْ المَعْرُوْف

A : Vocabulary:

اِجْتَنَبَ	نَصَرَ
He refrained.	He helped.

B : Definitions:

1.) مَنْفِيْ/نَفِي - The negative - where an action does not take place e.g. مَاضَرَبَ He did not hit i.e. The action of hitting did not take place. مَانَصَرَ He did not help.

C : Conjugation:

He did not do	وَاحِدْ مُذَكَّرْ غَائِبْ	مَافَعَلَ
They (2 men) did not do	تَثْنِيَهْ مُذَكَّرْ غَائِبْ	مَافَعَلَا
They (many men) did not do	جَمَعْ مُذَكَّرْ غَائِبْ	مَافَعَلُوْا
She did not do	وَاحِدْ مُؤَنَّثْ غَائِبْ	مَافَعَلَتْ
They (2 women) did not do	تَثْنِيَهْ مُؤَنَّثْ غَائِبْ	مَافَعَلَتَا
They (many women) did not do	جَمَعْ مُؤَنَّثْ غَائِبْ	مَافَعَلْنَ
You (1 man) did not do	وَاحِدْ مُذَكَّرْ حَاضِرْ	مَافَعَلْتَ
You (2 men) did not do	تَثْنِيَهْ مُذَكَّرْ حَاضِرْ	مَافَعَلْتُمَا
(All) you men did not do	جَمَعْ مُذَكَّرْ حَاضِرْ	مَافَعَلْتُمْ
You (1 woman) did not do	وَاحِدْ مُؤَنَّثْ حَاضِرْ	مَافَعَلْتِ
You (2 women) did not do	تَثْنِيَهْ مُؤَنَّثْ حَاضِرْ	مَافَعَلْتُمَا
(All) you women did not do	جَمَعْ مُؤَنَّثْ حَاضِرْ	مَافَعَلْتُنَّ
I did not do	وَاحِدْ مُذَكَّرْ وَمُؤَنَّثْ مُتَكَلِّمْ	مَافَعَلْتُ
We did not do	تَثْنِيَهْ وَجَمَعْ، مُذَكَّرْ وَمُؤَنَّثْ مُتَكَلِّمْ	مَافَعَلْنَا

* The addition of مَا before a word merely transforms it from positive to negative.

D: Exercises:

1.) Draw up the conjugation tables of the following:

a.) مَا نَصَرَ **b.)** مَااجْتَنَبَ with translation

c.) فَتَحَ **d.)** مَا تَرَكَ without translation

2.) Translate into English and write the segha (form) and بحث **(subject) thereof:**

a.) مَا فَعَلْتُنَّ b.) مَا ضَرَبْنَا c.) مَا اجْتَنَبْتَ d.) سَمِعْنَ

e.) مَا كَتَبْتُمَا f.) مَا اِجْتَنَبُوْا g.) مَا ضَرَبَا h.) سَمِعْنَا

3.) Translate into Arabic and write the segha (form) and بحث **(subject) thereof:**

a.) I did not hear.

b.) You two men did not refrain.

c.) Those two women hit.

d.) We wrote.

e.) He did not help.

f.) All you men helped.

g.) You one man did not refrain.

h.) You one woman refrained.

4.) Define:

a.) نَفِي b.) المَعْرُوْف c.) اِثْبَاتْ d.) مُتَكَلِّمْ e.) مَاضِيْ f.) غَائِب

5.) Identify all the past tense verbs and write the seghas (form) and بحث **(subject) thereof.**

١) ﴿قَالَتْ رَبِّ اِنِّيْ ظَلَمْتُ نَفْسِيْ وَاَسْلَمْتُ﴾ (سورة النمل: ٤٤)

٢) ﴿وَمَكَرُوْا مَكْرًا وَّمَكَرْنَا مَكْرًا﴾ (سورة النمل: ٥٠)

٣) ﴿وَاَنْجَيْنَا الَّذِيْنَ اٰمَنُوْا﴾ (سورة النمل: ٥٣)

٤) ﴿لِوَلِيِّهٖ مَاشَهِدْنَا مَهْلِكَ﴾ (سورة النمل: ٤٩)

٥) ﴿وَمَاخَلَقْتُ الْجِنَّ﴾ (سورة الذاريات: ٥٦)

٦) ﴿مَاعَلِمْتُ لَكُمْ مِنْ اِلٰهٍ غَيْرِيْ﴾ (سورة القصص: ٣٨)

٧) ﴿فَمَااسْتَطَاعُوْا مُضِيًّا وَّلَايَرْجِعُوْنَ﴾ (سورة يٰس: ٦٧)

LESSON 4
PAST PERFECT POSITIVE PASSIVE VERB

البحث: اَلْفِعْلُ المَاضِيْ المُثْبِتُ المَجْهُوْل

A : Vocabulary:

قَتَلَ	تَرَكَ
He killed.	He left.

B : Definitions:

1.) مَجْهُوْل : a passive verb - where the doer is unknown e.g. فُعِلَ He / It was done قُتِلَ He was killed.

The act of killing took place on him and we are not aware of WHO committed the crime.

2.) اَلْحُرُوْفُ الأَصْلِيَّة : the original or root letters. This refers to all those letters that fall parallel to ف, ع and ل .

Explanation:

The letter that appears in place of ف is called the ف kalima (first radical). The letter that appears in place of the ع is called the ع kalima (middle radical). The letter that appears in place of ل is called the ل kalima (final radical).

E.g. 1. In the word سَمِعَ the س is in place of the ف thus it is called the ف kalima. م is in place of the ع thus it is called the ع kalima. ع is in place of the ل thus it is called the ل kalima.

e.g.2:. (قَتَلَ)

a.) ق is the ف kalima (first radical.)

b.) ت is the ع kalima (middle radical.)

c.) ل is the ل kalima (final radical.)

3.) اَلْحُرُوْفُ الزَّائِدَة : (extra letters) all the letters besides those that fall parallel to ف ، ع and ل are regarded as extra letters or اَلْحُرُوْفُ الزَّائِدَة

e.g. اِجْتَنَبَ appears on the scale of اِفْتَعَلَ , thus the original letters will be ج ، ن and ب . The extra letters will be ا and ت .

e	d	c	b	a
ب	ن	ت	ج	ا
ل	ع	ت	ف	ا
e	d	c	b	a

a and c = extra letters - b, d and e = original letters.

b = ف kalima (first radical)

d = ع kalima (middle radical)

e = ل kalima (final radical)

4.) حَرْكَتْ - Short vowel i.e. kasra, dhamma, fatha (ـُــ ـِــ ـَــ)

C : Conjugation:

He (1 man) was done upon	وَاحِدْ مُذَكَّرْ غَائِبْ	فُعِلَ
They (2 men) were done upon	تَثْنِيَهْ مُذَكَّرْ غَائِبْ	فُعِلَا
They (all men) were done upon	جَمْعْ مُذَكَّرْ غَائِبْ	فُعِلُوْا
She was done upon	وَاحِدْ مُؤَنَّثْ غَائِبْ	فُعِلَتْ
They (2 women) were done upon	تَثْنِيَهْ مُؤَنَّثْ غَائِبْ	فُعِلَتَا
They (all women) were done upon	جَمْعْ مُؤَنَّثْ غَائِبْ	فُعِلْنَ
You (1 man) was done upon	وَاحِدْ مُذَكَّرْ حَاضِرْ	فُعِلْتَ
You (2 men) were done upon	تَثْنِيَهْ مُذَكَّرْ حَاضِرْ	فُعِلْتُمَا
(All) you men were done upon	جَمْعْ مُذَكَّرْ حَاضِرْ	فُعِلْتُمْ
You (1 woman) was done upon	وَاحِدْ مُؤَنَّثْ حَاضِرْ	فُعِلْتِ
You (2 women) were done upon	تَثْنِيَهْ مُؤَنَّثْ حَاضِرْ	فُعِلْتُمَا
(All) you women were done upon	جَمْعْ مُؤَنَّثْ حَاضِرْ	فُعِلْتُنَّ
I was done upon	وَاحِدْ مُذَكَّرْ وَمُؤَنَّثْ مُتَكَلِّمْ	فُعِلْتُ
We were done upon	تَثْنِيَهْ وَجَمْعْ، مُذَكَّرْ وَمُؤَنَّثْ مُتَكَلِّمْ	فُعِلْنَا

The method of making مَاضِىْ مَجْهُوْل (past passive)

1.) مَاضِىْ مَجْهُوْل is made from مَاضِىْ مَعْرُوْف in the following manner:

a.) Leave the لَام كَلِمَهْ and whatever is after it as it is e.g. قَتَلْتُ

b.) Change the عَيْن كَلِمَهْ into a kasra if it does not already have a kasra. e.g. قَتِلْتُ

c.) Give the فَا كَلِمَهْ and all the remaining letters which have a harkat a dhamma. e.g. قُتِلْتُ

Note: If a letter has a sukoon (jazm) then it should be left as it is . E.g. in. أُجْتُنِبَ

2.) The seghas will be the same as those in the مَعْرُوْف conjugation.

Exersises:

1.) Draw up the passive conjugation table of:

a.) تَرَكَ **b.)** قَتَلَ **c.)** اِجْتَنَبَ with translation

d.) سَمِعَ **e.)** نَصَرَ without translation

2.) Translate and write the form and topic for the following:

a.) نُصِرْنَا b.) تُرِكْتُ c.) قُتِلْتُ d.) أُجْتُنِبُوْا e.) سُمِعْتُمْ

f.) كَتَبَتَا g.) ضُرِبْتُمَا h.) نُصِرْنَ i.) أُجْتُنِبَتْ J.) قَتَلْتُ

3.) Write the Arabic of the following:

a.) All those men wrote.
b.) All those women were killed.
c.) I left.
d.) I was left.
e.) We killed.
f.) We were killed.
g.) You (2 men) helped.
h.) You (2 men) were killed.
i.) All you women heard.
J.) All you women refrained.
k.) You one woman refrained.
l.) You one woman was refrained from.

4.) Define:

a.) مَجْهُوْل b.) اَلْحُرُوْفُ الأَصْلِيَّة c.) اَلْحُرُوْفُ الزَّائِدَة d.) حَرْكَتْ

5.) Identify the active and passive verbs in the following aayaat:

١) ﴿ وَلَقَدْ جِئْتُمُوْنَا فُرٰدٰى كَمَا خَلَقْنٰكُمْ اَوَّلَ مَرَّةٍ وَّتَرَكْتُمْ ﴾ (سورة الانعام: ٩٤)

٢) ﴿ وَخُلِقَ الْإِنْسَانُ ضَعِيْفًا ﴾ (سورة النساء: ٢٨)

٣)﴿ فَاسْتَمْتَعْتُمْ بِخَلَاقِكُمْ كَمَا اسْتَمْتَعَ الَّذِيْنَ مِنْ قَبْلِكُمْ بِخَلَاقِهِمْ وَخُضْتُمْ كَالَّذِى خَاضُوْا اُولٰئِكَ حَبِطَتْ ﴾ (سورة التوبة: ٦٩)

٤) ﴿ فَلَمَّا رَأَيْنَهٗ اَكْبَرْنَهٗ وَقَطَّعْنَ ﴾ (سورة يوسف: ٣١)

٥)﴿ فَلَمَّا سَمِعَتْ بِمَكْرِهِنَّ اَرْسَلَتْ اِلَيْهِنَّ ﴾ (سورة يوسف: ٣١)

LESSON 5

CHAPTER ON THE POSITIVE ACTIVE VERB INCORPORATING THE PRESENT AND FUTURE TENSES (IMPERFECT)

بحث اَلْفِعْلِ الْمُضَارِعُ المَعْرُوْف المُثْبَت

A : Vocabulary:

حَمَلَ	جَلَسَ	فَتَحَ
He carried.	He sat.	He opened.

B : Definitions:

1.) مُضَارِع - refers to a present or future tense verb. e.g. يَضْرِبُ He is hitting or will hit.
يَفْتَحُ He is opening or will open.

2.) مَفْتُوْح - A word ending with a fatha.

3.) مَكْسُوْر - A word ending with a kasra.

4.) مَضْمُوْم - A word ending with a dhamma.

C : Conjugation:

He (1 man) is doing or will do	وَاحِدْ مُذَكَّرْ غَائِبْ	يَفْعَلُ
They (2 men) are doing or will do	تَثْنِيَهْ مُذَكَّرْ غَائِبْ	يَفْعَلَانِ
They (many men) are doing or will do	جَمْعْ مُذَكَّرْ غَائِبْ	يَفْعَلُوْنَ
She (1 woman) is doing or will do	وَاحِدْ مُؤَنَّثْ غَائِبْ	تَفْعَلُ
They (2 women) are doing or will do	تَثْنِيَهْ مُؤَنَّثْ غَائِبْ	تَفْعَلَانِ
They (many women) are doing or will do	جَمْعْ مُؤَنَّثْ غَائِبْ	يَفْعَلْنَ
You (1 man) are doing or will do	وَاحِدْ مُذَكَّرْ حَاضِرْ	تَفْعَلُ
You (2 men) are doing or will do	تَثْنِيَهْ مُذَكَّرْ حَاضِرْ	تَفْعَلَانِ
(All) you men are doing or will do	جَمْعْ مُذَكَّرْ حَاضِرْ	تَفْعَلُوْنَ
You (1 woman) are doing or will do	وَاحِدْ مُؤَنَّثْ حَاضِرْ	تَفْعَلِيْنَ
You (2 women) are doing or will do	تَثْنِيَهْ مُؤَنَّثْ حَاضِرْ	تَفْعَلَانِ
(All) you women are doing or will do	جَمْعْ مُؤَنَّثْ حَاضِرْ	تَفْعَلْنَ
I am doing or will do	وَاحِدْ مُذَكَّرْ و مُؤَنَّثْ مُتَكَلِّم	اَفْعَلُ
We are doing or will do	تَثْنِيَهْ وَجَمْعْ مُذَكَّرْومُؤَنَّثْ مُتَكَلِّم	نَفْعَلُ

Rules of making مُضَارِعْ مَعْرُوْف مُثْبَت

1.) To create مُضَارِع add one of the following letters to the beginning of مَاضِيْ : ا ، ت ، ى ، ن They are collectively read as اَتَيْن . These four letters are called عَلَامَاتُ الْمُضَارِع or the 'signs of مُضَارِع .
Alif appears in one segha only i.e. singular first person وَاحِدْ مُتَكَلِّمْ e.g. اَفْعَلُ

Noon appears in only one segha i.e. dual or plural first person جَمَعْ مُتَكَلِّمْ e.g. نَفْعَلُ
Yaa appears in four seghas, i.e three seghas of masculine third person.
e.g.

يَفْعَلُ	وَاحِدْ مُذَكَّرْ غَائِبْ
يَفْعَلَانِ	تَثْنِيَهْ مُذَكَّرْ غَائِبْ
يَفْعَلُوْنَ	جَمَعْ مُذَكَّرْ غَائِبْ

And the one segha of plural, feminine, third person e.g.

يَفْعَلْنَ	جَمَعْ مُؤَنَّثْ غَائِبْ

Taa appears in eight seghas, i.e the three masculine third person (مُذَكَّرْ حَاضِرْ) forms.

تَفْعَلُ	وَاحِدْ مُذَكَّرْ حَاضِرْ
تَفْعَلَانِ	تَثْنِيَهْ مُذَكَّرْ حَاضِرْ
تَفْعَلُوْنَ	جَمَعْ مُذَكَّرْ حَاضِرْ

Two in the feminine, third person (مُؤَنَّثْ غَائِبْ) seghas

تَفْعَلُ	وَاحِدْ مُؤَنَّثْ غَائِبْ
تَفْعَلَانِ	تَثْنِيَهْ مُؤَنَّثْ غَائِبْ

And the three in the feminine, second person seghas

تَفْعَلِيْنَ	وَاحِدْ مُؤَنَّثْ حَاضِرْ
تَفْعَلَانِ	تَثْنِيَهْ مُؤَنَّثْ حَاضِرْ
تَفْعَلْنَ	جَمَعْ مُؤَنَّثْ حَاضِرْ

2.) Five seghas of مُضَارِع will have a dhamma at the end.

يَفْعَلُ ، تَفْعَلُ ، تَفْعَلُ ، اَفْعَلُ ، نَفْعَلُ

Seven seghas of will have a "ن" اِعْرَابِيْ (Noon following a long vowel):

a.) The four dual seghas. In these four the noon will be maksoor.

يَفْعَلَانِ ، تَفْعَلَانِ ، تَفْعَلَانِ ، تَفْعَلَانِ

b.) The two masculine plurals of the second person (حَاضِرْ) and 3rd person (غَائِبْ) e.g. يَفْعَلُوْنَ ، تَفْعَلُوْنَ

c.) The one singular, feminine, second person. (وَاحِدْمُؤَنَّثْ حَاضِر) E.g تَفْعَلِيْنَ

In the last three (b and c) the noon will be مَفْتُوْح

3.) Just as the noon of جَمْع مُؤَنَّث appears in the past tense verbs e.g. فَعَلْنَ so too, does it appear in مُضَارِع i.e. يَفْعَلْنَ and تَفْعَلْنَ . It is among the مَبْنِى الْأَصل (Indeclinable words) and is also called noon dhameer. ("ن" ضَمِيْر)

4.) The present and future tense verbs are termed imperfect because they express an incomplete action.

For example:
Present tense: he is doing (action unfinished)
Future tense: he will do (action unfinished).

Exercises:

1.) Make the conjugations (گردان) of:

He Sat He Killed

a.) يَسْمَعُ b.) يَفْتَحُ c.) جَلَسَ d.) قَتَلَ e.) يَجْتَنِبُ

2.) Give the translation, form (segha) and subject (بحث) of the following words:

a.) يَتْرُكُ b.) اَقْتُلُ c.) نُصِرَ d.) تَضْرِبْنَ e.) تَسْمَعُ

f.) تَكْتُبُوْنَ g.) فَتَحْنَا h.) أُجْتُنِبَتْ i.) نَجْلِسُ j.) تَضْرِبِيْنَ

3.) Translate into Arabic:

a.) They (all men) are living.
b.) She is sitting.
c.) You two men are writing.
d.) All you women will hit.
e.) We opened.
f.) I am sitting.
g.) They (all women) were heard.
h.) We will refrain.
i.) You one woman will refrain.
j.) All you men were hit.

4.) Define:

a.) اَلْفِعْلُ الْمُضَارِعُ

5.) Choose all the مُضَارِع and مَاضِيْ words and also write down their seghas and بحث .

١) ﴿قَدْ سَمِعَ اللّٰهُ قَوْلَ الَّتِيْ تُجَادِلُكَ﴾ (سورة المجادلة: ١)

٢) ﴿لَا اَعْبُدُ الَّذِىْ فَطَرَنِيْ﴾ (سورة يٰس: ٢٢)

٣) ﴿وَمَا خَلَقْتُ الْجِنَّ وَالْاِنْسَ اِلَّا لِيَعْبُدُوْنِ﴾ (سورةا لذاريات: ٥٦)

٤) ﴿تَأْمُرُوْنَ بِالْمَعْرُوْفِ وَتَنْهوْنَ عَنِ الْمُنْكَرِ وَتُؤْمِنُوْنَ بِاللّٰهِ﴾ (سورة آل عمران: ١١٠)

LESSON 6

PRESENT AND FUTURE TENSE, POSITIVE, PASSIVE VERB

البحث الفِعْلُ الْمُضَارِع الْمُثْبِت الْمَجْهُوْل

A : Vocabulary:

ضَحِكَ	شَرِبَ	اَكَلَ
He laughed.	He drank.	He ate.

B : Conjugation:

He / it is being done	وَاحِدْ مُذَكَّرْ غَائِبْ	يُفْعَلُ
They (2 men) are being done	تَثْنِيَهْ مُذَكَّرْ غَائِبْ	يُفْعَلَانِ
They (all men) are being done	جَمَعْ مُذَكَّرْ غَائِبْ	يُفْعَلُوْنَ
She / it is being done	وَاحِدْ مُؤَنَّثْ غَائِبْ	تُفْعَلُ
They (2 women) are being done	تَثْنِيَهْ مُؤَنَّثْ غَائِبْ	تُفْعَلَانِ
They (all women) are being done	جَمَعْ مُؤَنَّثْ غَائِبْ	يُفْعَلْنَ
You (1 man) are being done	وَاحِدْ مُذَكَّرْ حَاضِرْ	تُفْعَلُ
You (2 men) are being done	تَثْنِيَهْ مُذَكَّرْ حَاضِرْ	تُفْعَلَانِ
(All) you men are being done	جَمَعْ مُذَكَّرْ حَاضِرْ	تُفْعَلُوْنَ
You (1 woman) are being done	وَاحِدْ مُؤَنَّثْ حَاضِرْ	تُفْعَلِيْنَ
You (2 women) are being done	تَثْنِيَهْ مُؤَنَّثْ حَاضِرْ	تُفْعَلَانِ
(All) you women are being done	جَمَعْ مُؤَنَّثْ حَاضِرْ	تُفْعَلْنَ
I am being done	وَاحِدْ مُذَكَّرْ و مُؤَنَّثْ مُتَكَلِّمْ	أُفْعَلُ
We are being done	تَثْنِيَهْ وَجَمَعْ، مُذَكَّرْوَمُؤَنَّثْ مُتَكَلِّمْ	نُفْعَلُ

The English translation of this verb may sound odd; however, it should be borne in mind that the dhameer does not have to pertain only to human beings. Hence, يُفْعَلُ could be translated as: it is being done. e.g. يُفْعَلُ الْأَمْرُ The work is being done.

Rules of making مُضَارِعْ مَعْرُوْف **(active) into** مُضَارِعْ مَجْهُوْل **(passive):**

1.) Give the عَلَامَت الْمُضَارِع (sign of mudhaarie) either, ا ، ت ، ي or ن a dhamma (pesh).

2.) Give the ع Kalima, (which is generally the second last letter in singular, masculine 3rd person i.e. يُفْعَلُ) a fatha if it does not already have one.

E.g.	يَفْعَلُ to يُفْعَلُ	يَجْتَنِبُ to يُجْتَنَبُ	يُكْرِمُ to يُكْرَمُ

Exercises:

1.) Draw up the passive conjugation table of:

a.) يَضْحَكُ With translation
b.) يَأْكُلُ With translation
C.) يَسْتَنْصِرُ Without translation

2.) write out the segha (form) بحث (subject) and translation of the following:

a.) يُشْرَبْنَ b.) أُضْرَبُ c.) تُسْمَعُوْنَ d.) تُفْتَحُ e.) أُجْتُنِبْتَا

f.) تُقْتَلِيْنَ g.) تَأْكُلُ h.) جَلَسْتُمَا i.) يُضْحَكُوْنَ j.) تُنْصَرَانِ

3.) Translate into Arabic:

a.) She is being laughed at.
b.) He was eaten.
c.) You two men are being left.
d.) They (all men) are being killed.
e.) You (one woman) are writing.

4.) Write the Arabic of the following:

a.) تَثْنِيَهْ مُؤَنَّثْ حَاضِرْ مَجْهُوْل of يَجْمَعُ
b.) جَمَعْ مُؤَنَّثْ غَائِبْ مَجْهُوْل of يَمْنَعُ
c.) جَمَعْ مُذَكَّرْ حَاضِرْ مَجْهُوْل of يَغْسِلُ
d.) وَاحِدْ مُؤَنَّثْ حَاضِرْ مَجْهُوْل of يَتْرُكُ
e.) جَمَعْ مُذَكَّرْومُؤَنَّثْ مُتَكَلِّمْ مَجْهُوْل of يَظْلِمُ

5.) Convert the following into مَجْهُوْل and state whether the word is مَاضِيْ or مُضَارِع :

a.) عَلِمَ b.) يَتَبَسَّمُ c.) يَشْهَدُ d.) تَسَرْبَلَ e.) اِجْتَنَبَ

f.) يُقَنْطِرُ g.) يَسْتَغْفِرُ h.) دَحْرَجَ i.) صَرَّفَ j.) يَحْتَمِلُ

LESSON 7
NEGATIVE PRESENT AND FUTURE TENSE ACTIVE AND PASSIVE VERB

البحث: نَفِي الفِعْلِ المُضَارِعِ المَعْرُوْفِ والمَجْهُوْلِ

A : Vocabulary:

اَكْرَمَ	غَسَلَ	مَنَعَ
He honoured.	He washed.	He prevented.

B : Conjugation:

اَلْبَحْثُ نَفِي الفِعْلِ الْمُضَارِعِ المَعْرُوْفِ

He is not doing or will not do	وَاحِدْ مُذَكَّرْ غَائِبْ	لَا يَفْعَلُ
They (2 men) are not doing or will not do	تَثْنِيَهْ مُذَكَّرْ غَائِبْ	لَا يَفْعَلَانِ
They (all men) is not doing or will not do	جَمْعْ مُذَكَّرْ غَائِبْ	لَا يَفْعَلُوْنَ
She (1 women) is not doing or will not do	وَاحِدْ مُؤَنَّثْ غَائِبْ	لَا تَفْعَلُ
They (2 women) are not doing or will not do	تَثْنِيَهْ مُؤَنَّثْ غَائِبْ	لَا تَفْعَلَانِ
They (all women) are not doing or will not do	جَمْعْ مُؤَنَّثْ غَائِبْ	لَا يَفْعَلْنَ
You (1 man) are not doing or will not do	وَاحِدْ مُذَكَّرْ حَاضِرْ	لَا تَفْعَلُ
You (2 men) are not doing or will not do	تَثْنِيَهْ مُذَكَّرْ حَاضِرْ	لَا تَفْعَلَانِ
(All) you men are not doing or will not do	جَمْعْ مُذَكَّرْ حَاضِرْ	لَا تَفْعَلُوْنَ
You (1 woman) are not doing or will not do	وَاحِدْ مُؤَنَّثْ حَاضِرْ	لَا تَفْعَلِيْنَ
You (2 women) are not doing or will not do	تَثْنِيَهْ مُؤَنَّثْ حَاضِرْ	لَا تَفْعَلَانِ
All you women are not doing and will not do	جَمْعْ مُؤَنَّثْ حَاضِرْ	لَا تَفْعَلْنَ
I am not doing or will not do	وَاحِدْ مُذَكَّرْ و مُؤَنَّثْ مُتَكَلِّمْ	لَا اَفْعَلُ
We are not doing or will not do	تَثْنِيَهْ وَجَمْعْ، مُذَكَّرْ وَمُؤَنَّثْ مُتَكَلِّمْ	لَا نَفْعَلُ

C : Conjugation: البحث نَفي الفِعْلِ المُضَارِعِ المَجْهُوْل

He/ It is not being done or will not be done	وَاحِدْ مُذَكَّرْ غَائِبْ	لَايُفْعَلُ
They (2 men) are not being done or will not be done	تَثْنِيَهْ مُذَكَّرْ غَائِبْ	لَايُفْعَلَانِ
They (many men) are not being done or will not be done	جَمْعْ مُذَكَّرْ غَائِبْ	لَايُفْعَلُوْنَ
She/ It (1 woman) is not being done or will not be done	وَاحِدْ مُؤَنَّثْ غَائِبْ	لَاتُفْعَلُ
They (2 women) are not being done or will not be done	تَثْنِيَهْ مُؤَنَّثْ غَائِبْ	لَاتُفْعَلَانِ
They (many women) are not being done or will not be done	جَمْعْ مُؤَنَّثْ غَائِبْ	لَايُفْعَلْنَ
You (1 man) are not being done or will not be done	وَاحِدْ مُذَكَّرْ حَاضِرْ	لَاتُفْعَلُ
You (2 men) are not being done or will not be done	تَثْنِيَهْ مُذَكَّرْ حَاضِرْ	لَاتُفْعَلَانِ
(All) you men are not being done or will not be done	جَمْعْ مُذَكَّرْ حَاضِرْ	لَاتُفْعَلُوْنَ
You (1 woman) are not being done or will not be done	وَاحِدْ مُؤَنَّثْ حَاضِرْ	لَاتُفْعَلِيْنَ
You (2 women) are not being done or will not be done	تَثْنِيَهْ مُؤَنَّثْ حَاضِرْ	لَاتُفْعَلَانِ
(All) you women are not being done or will not be done	جَمْعْ مُؤَنَّثْ حَاضِرْ	لَاتُفْعَلْنَ
I am not being done or will not be done	وَاحِدْ مُذَكَّرْ و مُؤَنَّثْ مُتَكَلِّمْ	لَاأُفْعَلُ
We are not being done or will not be done	تَثْنِيَهْ وَجَمْعْ، مُذَكَّرْوَمُؤَنَّثْ مُتَكَلِّمْ	لَانُفْعَلُ

The addition of لَا before a word merely transforms it from positive to negative.

D : Exercises:

1.) Draw up the conjugation table of:

a.) بحث نَفي الفِعْلِ المُضَارِعِ المَعْرُوْف of غَسَلَ

b.) بحث نَفي الفِعْلِ المُضَارِعِ المَجْهُوْل of مَنَعَ

2.) Translate into English and write the segha (form) and بحث (subject) of the following:

a.) لَايَمْنَعْنَ b.) لَاتَسْمَعِيْنَ c.) لَايُضْرَبُوْنَ d.) لَاتُغْسَلَانِ e.) مَامُنِعَتْ

f.) مَاضَحِكْنَا g.) يَكْتُبْنَ h.) لَاتَتْرُكُ i.) لَاتُقْتَلُ j.) لَاتُجْتَنَبُوْنَ

3.) Translate into Arabic:

a.) I will not eat.
b.) She will not be prevented.
c.) You one man was not left.
d.) He drank.
e.) You one woman will not be laughed at.

4). Chose all the verbs and write down the segha (form) and بحث (subject) thereof:

١) ﴿ لَا اَعْبُدُ مَا تَعْبُدُوْنَ ﴾ (سورة الكافرون: ٢)

٢) ﴿ وَرَأَيْتَ النَّاسَ يَدْخُلُوْنَ فِيْ دِيْنِ اللهِ اَفْوَاجًا ﴾ (سورة النصر: ٢)

٣) ﴿ اَلَّذِيْنَ هُمْ يُرَاءُوْنَ وَيَمْنَعُوْنَ الْمَاعُوْنَ ﴾ (سورة الماعون: ٦، ٧)

٤) ﴿ اَلَّذِيْنَ يُوْمِنُوْنَ بِالْغَيْبِ وَيُقِيْمُوْنَ الصَّلٰوةَ وَمِمَّا رَزَقْنٰهُمْ يُنْفِقُوْنَ ﴾ (سورة البقرة:٣)

٥) ﴿ يُخَادِعُوْنَ اللهَ وَالَّذِيْنَ اٰمَنُوْا وَمَا يَخْدَعُوْنَ اِلَّا اَنْفُسَهُمْ وَمَا يَشْعُرُوْنَ ﴾ (سورة البقرة: ٩)

٦) ﴿ كُلَّمَا اُلْقِيَ فِيْهَا فَوْجٌ سَأَلَهُمْ خَزَنَتُهَا ﴾ (سورة الملك: ٨)

٧) ﴿ قَالُوْا بَلٰى قَدْ جَاءَنَا نَذِيْرٌ فَكَذَّبْنَا وَقُلْنَا مَا نَزَّلَ اللهُ مِنْ شَيْءٍ ﴾ (سورة الملك: ٩)

٨) ﴿ فَاِذَا نُفِخَ فِى الصُّوْرِ ﴾ (سورة المؤمنون: ١٠١)

٩) ﴿ فَلَا يَسْتَطِيْعُوْنَ تَوْصِيَةً وَّلَا اِلَى اَهْلِهِمْ يَرْجِعُوْنَ ﴾ (سورة يٰس: ٥٠)

١٠) ﴿ فَالْيَوْمَ لَا تُظْلَمُ نَفْسٌ شَيْئًا ﴾ (سورة يٰس: ٥٤)

١١) ﴿ هٰذِهِ جَهَنَّمُ الَّتِيْ كُنْتُمْ تُوْعَدُوْنَ ﴾ (سورة يٰس: ٦٣)

١٢) ﴿ اَلْيَوْمَ نَخْتِمُ عَلٰى اَفْوَاهِهِمْ وَتُكَلِّمُنَا اَيْدِيْهِمْ وَتَشْهَدُ اَرْجُلُهُمْ بِمَا كَانُوْا يَكْسِبُوْنَ ﴾ (سورة يٰس ٦٣)

LESSON 8
DIVISION OF THE VERB INTO SIX GROUPS

A baab (group / category) is formed when the وَاحِدْ مُذَكَّر غَائِب of مَاضِى and the وَاحِدْ مُذَكَّر غَائِب of مُضَارِع are put together and read. As far as verbs are concerned there are altogether twenty four categories. We will deal with only six in this lesson.

	SCALE	EXAMPLE	NAME OF SCALE	ABBR.
1	فَعَلَ يَفْعُلُ	عَبَدَ يَعْبُدُ	نَصَرَ يَنْصُرُ	ن
2	فَعَلَ يَفْعِلُ	جَلَسَ يَجْلِسُ	ضَرَبَ يَضْرِبُ	ض
3	فَعِلَ يَفْعَلُ	عَلِمَ يَعْلَمُ	سَمِعَ يَسْمَعُ	س
4	فَعَلَ يَفْعَلُ	ذَهَبَ يَذْهَبُ	فَتَحَ يَفْتَحُ	ف
5	فَعُلَ يَفْعُلُ	كَبُرَ يَكْبُرُ	كَرُمَ يَكْرُمُ	ک
6	فَعِلَ يَفْعِلُ	نَعِمَ يَنْعِمُ	حَسِبَ يَحْسِبُ	ح

All words which consist of three original letters in the وَاحِدْ مُذَكَّر غَائِب of مَاضِىْ will appear on one of the above scales. If the harakaat of any word corresponds to the مَاضِى and مُضَارِع of any of the above then it will receive the name of that baab.
E.g. The word عَبَدَ is from baab (category) نَصَرَ يَنْصُرُ on the scale of فَعَلَ يَفْعُلُ

Note 1: Baab no.5 (كَرُمَ - يَكْرُمُ) is a laazim baab i.e. it does not receive the مَجْهُوْل seghas, e.g. the following is incorrect:

كُبِرَ يُكْبَرُ   كُرِمَ يُكْرَمُ

Note 2: The first three baabs are called أُمُّ الْاَبْوَاب i.e. The Primary Baabs because the middle radical(عَيْن كَلِمَة) of مَاضِىْ and مُضَارِع do not correspond. The last three are called فُرُوْعِى baabs, i.e. The Secondary Baabs, because the middle radical i.e. the عَيْن كَلِمَة of مَاضِىْ and مُضَارِع correspond.

Note 3: The most frequently used scales are the first three. The fourth scale is used less frequently, the fifth scale even less, and the sixth scale is the least used scale.

Exercise 1

1.1) Translate the following sentences.

1.2) Identify the مَاضِيْ مَعْرُوف and مَجْهُوْل and NOTE the difference.

1.3) Write the بحث and segha of each verb.

١)	هُوَ قَرَأَ الْقُرْآنَ	هُوَ قُرِأَ
٢)	قَرَأَ رَشِيْدُ الْقُرْآنَ	قُرِأَ الْقُرْآنُ
٣)	هُمَا(رَجُلَانِ) قَرَءَاكِتَابًا	هُمَا(رَجُلَانِ) طُلِبَا
٤)	هُمْ (الرِّجَالُ) قَرَأُوْا الْقُرْآنَ	هُمْ (الرِّجَالُ) طُلِبُوْا
٥)	هِيَ (بِنْتٌ) كَتَبَتْ مَكْتُوْبًا	هِيَ (بِنْتٌ) طُلِبَتْ
٦)	هُمَا(بِنْتَانِ) كَتَبَتَا مَكْتُوْبَيْنِ	هُمَا(بِنْتَانِ) طُلِبَتَا
٧)	هُنَّ (الْبَنَاتُ) كَتَبْنَ مَكَاتِبَ	هُنَّ (الْبَنَاتُ)طُلِبْنَ
٨)	أَنْتَ اَكَلْتَ تُفَّاحًا	اَنْتَ بُعِثْتَ إِلَى لَاهُوْر
٩)	أَنْتُمَا أَكَلْتُمَا رُمَّانًا	أَنْتُمَا بُعِثْتُمَا إِلَى كَرَاتْشِي
١٠)	أَنْتُمْ أَكَلْتُمْ بِطِّيْخًا	أَنْتُمْ بُعِثْتُمْ إِلَى مَكَّةَ
١١)	أَنْتِ طَلَبْتِ الْعِلْمَ	أَنْتِ بُعِثْتِ إِلَى الْمَدْرَسَةِ
١٢)	أَنْتُمَا طَلَبْتُمَا العِلْمَ	أَنْتُمَا بُعِثْتُمَا إِلَى الْبَيْتِ
١٣)	أَنْتُنَّ طَلَبْتُنَّ الْعِلْمَ	أَنْتُنَّ بُعِثْتُنَّ إِلَى الْمُسْتَشْفَى
١٤)	أَنَا شَرِبْتُ مَاءً	اَنَا بُعِثْتُ إِلَى الدِّهْلِيْ
١٥)	نَحْنُ شَرِبْنَا لَبَنًا	نَحْنُ بُعِثْنَا إِلَى كَلْكَتَّة
١٦)	يَارَشِيْدُ! هَلْ قَرَأْتَ الْقُرْآنَ ؟	نَعَمْ يَا سَيِّدِيْ! قَرَأْتُ جُزْءًا مِنْهُ
١٧)	هَلْ كَتَبْتَ الْمَكْتُوْبَ إِلَى أَبِيْكَ؟	نَعَمْ،كَتَبْتُ الْبَارِحَة
١٨)	مَتَى طَلَعَتِ الشَّمْسُ؟	مَاطَلَعَتِ الشَّمْسُ إِلَى الْآنَ
١٩)	هَلْ غَرَبَ الْقَمَرُ؟	نَعَمْ غَرَبَ الْقَمَرُ قَبْلَ سَاعَةٍ
٢٠)	مَاذَا أَكَلْتِ الْيَوْمَ يَا مَرْيَمُ؟	يَاسَيِّدِيْ أَكَلْتُ الْخُبْزَ مَعَ اللَّبَنِ
٢١)	إِلَى أَيْنَ بُعِثَ أَبُوْكَ؟	بُعِثَ أَبِيْ إِلَى اِلٰه آبَاد
٢٢)	مَنْ دَخَلَ الدَّارَ ؟	هِيَ أُمِّيْ دَخَلَتِ الدَّارَ
٢٣)	وَمَنْ خَرَجَ مِنْهَا ؟	هُمَا أَخَوَايَ قَدْ خَرَجَا مِنَ الدَّارِ
٢٤)	مَنْ ضَرَبَ أَخَوَيْكَ؟	ضَرَبَتْهُمَا أُمِّيْ
٢٥)	هَلْ فُتِحَ بَابُ الْمَدْرَسَةِ؟	لَا، مَا فُتِحَ إِلَى الْآنَ
٢٦)	لِمَ فَرِحَ مُحَمَّدٌ وَرَشِيْدٌ ؟	لِأَنَّهُمَا نَجَحَا فِي الْاِمْتِحَانِ

٢٧) كَمْ وَلَدًا نَجَحَ فِى الْإِمْتِحَانِ السَّنَوِىْ؟ — نَجَحَ خَمْسُوْنَ وَلَدًا فِيْ هٰذَا الْعَامِ

٢٨) هَلْ فَهِمْتُمْ قَوْلَنَا؟ — مَا فَهِمْنَا قَوْلَكُمْ

٢٩) لِمَ مَا فَهِمْتُمْ كَلَامِيْ؟ — لِأَنَّ لِسَانَكُمْ هِنْدِيٌّ

٣٠) لِمَ طُلِبْتَ فِى الدِّيْوَانِ؟ — طُلِبْتُ لِلشَّهَادَةِ

٣١) لِمَ بُعِثْتِ إِلَى الْمُسْتَشْفٰى يَا أُخْتِيْ؟ — بُعِثْتُ لِلتَّمْرِيْضِ (لِخِدْمَةِ الْمَرْضٰى)

From the Qur`aan

١) ﴿كَمْ مِنْ فِئَةٍ قَلِيْلَةٍ غَلَبَتْ فِئَةً كَثِيْرَةً بِإِذْنِ اللهِ﴾ (سورة البقرة: ٢٤٩)

٢) ﴿مَنْ قَتَلَ نَفْسًا بِغَيْرِ نَفْسٍ اَوْ فَسَادٍ فِى الْاَرْضِ فَكَاَنَّمَا قَتَلَ النَّاسَ جَمِيْعًا﴾ (سورة المائدة: ٣٢)

٣) ﴿كَمْ تَرَكُوْا مِن جَنّٰتٍ وَّعُيُوْنٍ وَزُرُوْعٍ وَمَقَامٍ كَرِيْمٍ﴾ (سورة الدخان: ٢٦)

٤) ﴿لِلرِّجَالِ نَصِيْبٌ مِمَّا تَرَكَ الْوَالِدَانِ وَالْاَقْرَبُوْنَ وَلِلنِّسَاءِ نَصِيْبٌ مِمَّا تَرَكَ الْوَالِدَانِ وَالْاَقْرَبُوْنَ﴾ (سورة النساء: ٧)

٥) ﴿فَمَنْ شَرِبَ مِنْهُ فَلَيْسَ مِنِّيْ﴾ (سورة البقرة: ٢٤٩)

٦) ﴿فَشَرِبُوْا مِنْهُ اِلَّا قَلِيْلًا مِّنْهُمْ﴾ (سورة البقرة: ٢٤٩)

٧) ﴿كُتِبَ عَلَيْكُمُ الصِّيَامُ كَمَا كُتِبَ عَلَى الَّذِيْنَ مِنْ قَبْلِكُمْ﴾ (سورة البقرة:١٨٣)

٨) ﴿وَاِذَا الْمَوْءُدَةُ سُئِلَتْ بِاَيِّ ذَنْبٍ قُتِلَتْ﴾ (سورة التكوير: ٩)

Exercise 2

2.1.) Translate the following sentences.
2.2.) Write the بحث and segha of each verb.

١) كَم مِنَ الْقُرْآن تَقْرَأُ كُلَّ يَوْمٍ يَا خَلِيْلُ؟ — كُلَّ يَوْمٍ أَقْرَأُ جُزْءً مِنْهُ لٰكِنِ الْيَوْمَ مَا قَرَأْتُ إِلَّا نِصْفَ الْجُزْءِ.

٢) لِمَا ذَا ؟ لِأَنِّيْ مَاكَتَبْتُ وَاجِبَاتِ الْمَدْرَسَةِ فِى اللَّيْلِ فَجَلَسْتُ أَكْتُبُ صَبَاحًا.

٣) هَلْ حَصَلَتْ لَكَ الْيَوْمَ جَمَاعَةُ الْفَجْرِ ؟ — اَلْحَمْدُ للهِ كُلَّ يَوْمٍ تَحْصِلُ لِيْ جَمَاعَةُ الْفَجْرِ.

٤) فَأَنْتَ ذُوْ حَظٍّ عَظِيْمٍ وَاللهِ يَاخَلِيْلُ — اَشْكُرُكَ يَاسَيِّدِىْ عَلَى حُسْنِ ظَنِّكَ أَمَّا جَمَاعَةُ الْفَجْرِ فَلَيْسَ بِأَمْرٍ كَبِيْرٍ إِلَّا عَلَى الْكُسَالٰى الَّذِيْنَ يَرْقُدُوْنَ فِى الْغَفْلَةِ.

٥) صَدَقْتَ يَا وَلَدِيْ وَلٰكِنْ لَيْسَ هٰذَا إِلَّا نَصِيْبُ السُّعَدَاءِ رَزَقَكَ اللهُ سَعَادَةَ الدَّارَيْنِ اٰمِيْن وَرَفَعَ اللهُ دَرَجَاتِ سَيِّدِيْ .

٦) يَاخَلِيْلُ! مَتَى تَذْهَبُ إِلَى الْمَدْرَسَةِ؟ — أَنَا أَذْهَبُ بَعْدَ الْفُطُوْرِ .

٧) وَمَتَى تَأْكُلُوْنَ الْغَدَاءَ ؟ — نَحْنُ نَأْكُلُ الْغَدَاءَ قَبْلَ الظُّهْرِ .

٨) اَلْمَدْرَسَةُ قَرِيْبَةٌ أَمْ بَعِيْدَةٌ ؟ — بَعُدَتِ الْمَدْرَسَةُ نَحْوَ نِصْفِ مِيْلٍ.

٩) هَلْ تَشْرَبُ الشَّايَ عِنْدَنَا ؟ — عَلَى الرَّأْسِ وَالْعَيْنِ ، وَلٰكِنْ يَاسَيِّدِىْ! أَنَا شَرِبْتُ الشَّايَ صَبَاحًا وَلَا أَشْرَبُ بَعْدَ ذٰلِكَ أَبَداً.

١٠) مَنْ هٰذَا الْوَلَدُ الصَّغِيْرُ مَعَكَ ؟ — هٰذَا وَلَدٌ يَسْكُنُ أَبَوَاهُ فِيْ جَارِنَا .

١١) لَيْسَ هُوَ بِنَظِيْفٍ أَلَا يُغْسَلُ وَجْهُهُ؟ — اَلْيَوْمَ مَرِضَتْ أُمُّهُ فَمَاغَسَلَتْ وَجْهَهُ.

١٢) هَلْ تَلْعَبُوْنَ كُلَّ يَوْمٍ بَعْدَ الْعَصْرِ ؟ — نَعَم نَلْعَبُ كُلَّ يَوْمٍ فِى الْمَيْدَانِ.

١٣) مَتَى تَرْجِعُ مِنَ الْمَيْدَانِ اللَّعِبِ؟ أَنَا أَرْجِعُ قُبَيْلَ الْمَغْرِبِ .

١٤) فَمَاذَا تَفْعَلُ ؟ بَعْدَ صَلوٰةِ الْمَغْرِبِ نَأْكُلُ الْعَشَاءَ وَنَسْمَعُ أَخْبَارَ الْعَالَمِ فِى الرَّادِيُوْ .

١٥) مَاذَا سَمِعْتَ الْبَارِحَةَ؟ يَا سَيِّدِىْ! سَمِعْتُ خَبَرًا مُدْهِشًا .

١٦) وَمَاذَاكَ ؟ سَمِعْتُ أَنَّ الْيَابَانَ قَدْ هَزَمَتِ الْبِرْطَانِيَةَ وَالْاَمْرِيْكَا فِىْ مَلَايَا وَبَرْمَاوَقَدْ قَرُبَتِ الْآنَ مِنَ الْهِنْدِ.

١٧) صَدَقْتَ يَا عَزِيْزِىْ! هٰكَذَا جَاءَتْ الْأَخْبَارُ فِى الْجَرَائِدِ أَيْضًا،حَفَظَنَا اللهُ مِنْ شَرِّ هٰذِهِ الْحَرْبِ الْمُخَرِّبَةِ .

Exercise 3

3.1) Translate the following.

3.2) Identify all verbs found in the following sentences and aayaat by writing the بحث and segha of each.

١) هَلْ تَفْهَمُ لِسَانَ الْعَرَبِيَّ ؟ نَعَمْ أَفْهَمُهُ قَلِيْلًا

٢) مَنْ يَكْتُبُ هٰذَا الْكِتَابَ ؟ تَكْتُبُهُ أُخْتِيْ مَرْيَمَ

٣) مَاشَاءَ اللهُ هِيَ تَكْتُبُ جَيِّدًا وَأَنْتَ لَا تَكْتُبُ يَاسَيِّدِىْ! أَنَا لَا أَكْتُبُ لِأَنَّ فِيْ يَدِيْ وَجْعٌ

٤) اِلٰى اينَ تَذْهَبُ يَا أَحْمَدُ ؟ أَنَا أَذْهَبُ إِلَى السُّوْقِ

٥) مَتَى تَرْجِعُ مِنَ السُّوْقِ؟ سَأَرْجِعُ مِنْهَا فِيْ سَاعَةٍ وَاحِدَةٍ

٦) يَا اَوْلَادُ! أَيُّ كِتَابٍ تَقْرَؤُنَ ؟ نَقْرَأُ تَسْهِيْلَ الْاَدَبِ

٧) هَلْ تَشْرَبُوْنَ الشَّايَ ؟ نَحْنَ لَا نَشْرَبُ الشَّايَ وَلَا الْقَهْوَةَ

٨) هَلْ بُعِثْتُمْ إِلَى الْحَاكِمِ الْيَوْمَ؟ لَا، بَلْ نُبْعَثُ غَدًا بَعْدَ الظُّهْرِ

٩) مَنْ طَلَبَكُمْ إِلَى بَمْبَائِيْ ؟ طَلَبَنَا أَبُوْنَا إِلَى بَمْبَائِيْ

١٠) هَلْ تَعْلَمُوْنَ مَنْ خَلَقَكُمْ وَوَالِدَيْكُمْ ؟ اَللّٰهُ خَلَقَنِيْ وَخَلَقَ وَالِدَيَّ

١١) مَاذَا تَطْلُبِيْنَ مِنَّا يَا عَائِشَةُ؟ إِنَّمَا أَطْلُبُ مِنْكُمْ كِتَابًا يَنْفَعُنِيْ

١٢) هَلْ رَأَيْتُمُوْنَا أَمْسِ فِى الْجَامِعِ؟ لَا،وَاللهِ! مَارَاَيْنَا كُمْ هُنَاكَ

١٣) هَلْ تَسْمَعُ أَخْبَارَ الْحَرْبِ فِى الرَّادِيُوْ؟ إِيْ وَاللهِ! أَسْمَعُ صَبَاحًا وَمَسَاءًا

١٤) وَهَلْ تَقْرَأُ الْجَرَائِدَ؟ كَيْفَ لَا أَقْرَأُهَا وَهِيَ مِنْ أَهَمِّ الْأُمُوْرِ

From the Qur`an

١) ﴿ وَلِلّٰهِ الْعِزَّةُ وَلِرَسُوْلِهِ وَلِلْمُؤْمِنِيْنَ وَلٰكِنَّ الْمُنَافِقِيْنَ لَا يَعْلَمُوْنَ ﴾ (سورة المنافقون: ٨)

٢) ﴿ لِيْ عَمَلِيْ وَلَكُمْ عَمَلُكُمْ اَنْتُمْ بَرِيْئُوْنَ مِمَّا اَعْمَلُ وَاَنَا بَرِيْءٌ مِمَّا تَعْمَلُوْنَ ﴾ (سورة يونس: ٤١)

٣) ﴿ اِنَّ اللهَ لَا يَظْلِمُ النَّاسَ شَيْئًا وَلٰكِنَّ النَّاسَ اَنْفُسَهُمْ يَظْلِمُوْنَ ﴾ (سورة يونس: ٤٤)

٤) ﴿ قُلْ لَّا اَمْلِكُ لِنَفْسِىْ ضَرًّا وَّلَا نَفْعًا ﴾ (سورة يونس: ٤٩)

٥) ﴿ اَلَّذِيْنَ يَاْكُلُوْنَ اَمْوَالَ الْيَتَامٰى ظُلْمًا اِنَّمَا يَأْكُلُوْنَ فِىْ بُطُوْنِهِمْ نَارًا ﴾ (سورة النساء: ١٠)

٦) ﴿ وَمَالِيَ لَا اَعْبُدُ الَّذِىْ فَطَرَنِىْ وَاِلَيْهِ تُرْجَعُوْنَ﴾ (سورة يٰس: ٢٢)

٧) ﴿ اَفَلَا يَنْظُرُوْنَ اِلَى الْاِبِلِ كَيْفَ خُلِقَتْ﴾ (سورة الغاشية: ١٧)

٨) ﴿ قُلْ يَا اَيُّهَا الْكَافِرُوْنَ لَا اَعْبُدُ مَا تَعْبُدُوْنَ وَ لَا اَنْتُمْ عَابِدُوْنَ مَا اَعْبُدُ وَلَا اَنَا عَابِدٌ مَّا عَبَدْتُّمْ وَ لَا اَنْتُمْ عَابِدُوْنَ مَا اَعْبُدُ لَكُمْ دِيْنُكُمْ وَلِيَ دِيْنِ﴾ (سورة الكافرون: ١- ٦)

٩) ﴿ لَايُسْاَلُ عَمَّا يَفْعَلُ وَهُمْ يُسْئَلُوْنَ﴾ (سورة الانبياء: ٢٣)

LESSON 9
CHAPTER ON THE PASSIVE VERB

اَلفِعْلُ المَجْهُوْلُ

A : Vocabulary:

عَذَرَ	سَمِحَ	مَنَحَ
He made an excuse.	He gave permission.	He gave.

B : Verbs are of two types:

1.) اَلفِعْلُ اللَّازِمُ (Intransitive verbs)-this refers to such a verb which does not require a مَفْعُوْلٌ to be complete. The sentence is complete with a فَاعِل alone

Eg. فَرِحَ زَيْدٌ Zaid was happy.
سَكَتَ حَامِدٌ Hamid was silent,
جَاءَ الْقَوْمُ The nation / people came.

2.) اَلفِعْلُ المَتَعَدِّي (Transitive verb) - this refers to a verb which requires a مَفْعُوْلٌ to be complete.

E.g أَكَلَ زَيْدٌ اَلخُبْزَ Zaid ate the bread.
قَتَلَ دَاوُدُ جَالُوْتَ Dawood killed Jaloot.

Some verbs require two مَفْعُوْل`s to be complete. They are called مُتَعَدِّىْ إِلَى المَفْعُوْلَيْنِ e.g. The following sentence has one mafool but the sentence is incomplete,

حَسِبَ زَيْدٌ عَمْرًوا Zaid thought Amr .... When the word غَنِيًّا is added as a second مَفْعُوْل then the sentence becomes complete.

حَسِبَ زَيْدٌ عَمْرًوا غَنِيًّا Zaid thought Amr was rich / Zaid considered Amr to be rich.

Transitive verbs are further divided into:

1.) مَعْرُوْف (active) and
2.) مَجْهُوْل (passive)

In active verbs the verb refers to the subject i.e. the doer (فَاعِل) of the action.
In passive verbs the verb refers to the object i.e. the مَفْعُوَل

قَتَلَ زَيْدٌ أَسَدًا Zaid killed a lion - active
قُتِلَ أَسَدٌ A lion was killed - passive

In the first sentence the verb refers to the فَاعِل because it is an active verb. In the second sentence the verb refers to the مَفْعُوْل because it is a passive verb. A فَاعِل receives a dhamma while a مَفْعُوْل takes on a fatha. In a passive sentence the مَفْعُوْل will be called مَفْعُوْلُ مَالَمْ يُسَمَّ فَاعِلُهُ or a نَائِبُ فَاعِل (substitute of a فَاعِل) and will therefore receive a dhamma.

The first مَفْعُوْل of those words that require two مَفْعُوْل `s will, in the passive (مَجْهُوْل) case, become the نَائِب فَاعِل and therefore be marfoo; whilst the other مَفْعُوْل will remain mansoob on the basis of being مَفْعُوْل .

Note : when there is no possibility of confusion then either of the two مَفْعُوْل`s can become the نَائِبُ فَاعِل
E.g. حُسِبَ عَمْرٌو غَنِيًّا - Amr was considered to be rich.

Diagram illustrating the division of verbs:

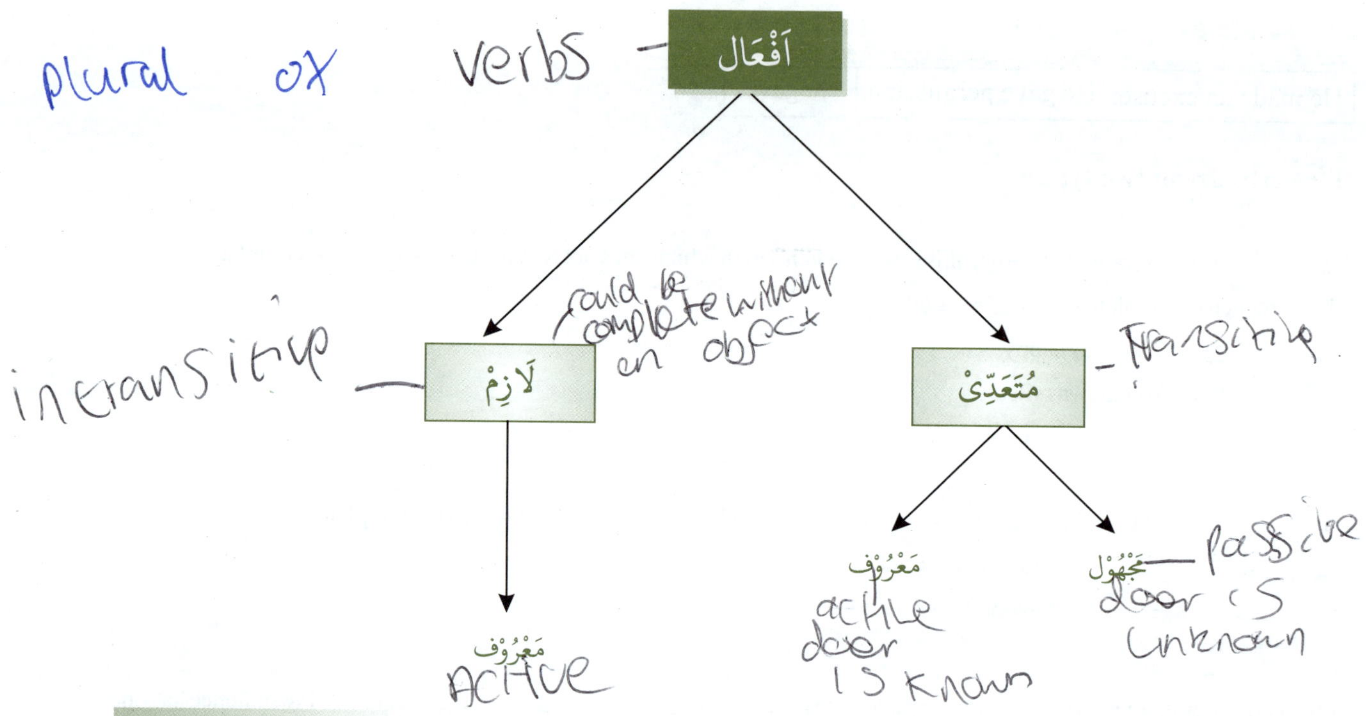

Exercise:

1a.) Translate the following sentences:

b.) If they are مَعْرُوْف convert them into مَجْهُوْل and if they are مَجْهُوْل convert them into مَعْرُوْف .

c.) Translate each sentence in its new form.

d.) State the segha (mood) and the بحث (topic) of each verb.

١) شَرِبَ الطِّفْلُ لَبَنًا

٢) طَلَبَ أَخُوكَ حَامِدٌ أَبَاكَ

٣) أَكَلْنَا الْيَوْمَ السَّمَكَ وَالْأَرُزَّ

٤) أَرْسَلَ حَامِدٌ أَخَاهُ إِلَى مِصْرَ

٥) هَلْ تَفْهَمُ أُخْتُكَ الْفَارِسِيَّ

٦) قَتَلَ عَسْكَرِيٌّ أَبَاهُ فِيْ مُحَارَبَةِ سِنْغَافُوْر

٧) قُتِلَ أَسَدٌ كَبِيْرٌ

٨) طُلِبَ أَبُوْكَ فِي الدِّيْوَانِ

٩) هَلْ فُتِحَ بَابُ الْمَدْرَسَةِ

١٠) نَعَمْ فَتَحَ الْبَوَّابُ بَابَ الْمَدْرَسَةِ

١١) قُتِلَ أَبُوْ هٰذَا الْوَلَدِ فِيْ مُحَارَبَةِ لِيْبِيَا

١٢) هَلْ يَفْهَمُ لِسَانُ الْهِنْدِيْ فِيْ مَكَّةَ؟

١٣) بُعِثَ أَخُوْهُ إِلَى حَيْدَرَآبَادْ

١٤) سَيُهْزَمُ الْكُفَّارُ

١٥) قَتَلَ دَاوُدُ جَالُوْتَ

١٦) حَسِبَتْ أَخَاكَ صَالِحًا

LESSON 10
CHAPTER ON THE USAGE OF لَنْ

بحث: نفيِ ب"لَنْ" درْ فِعل مُستقبِل مَعرُوف

A : Vocabulary:

أَسْلَمَ	عَبَدَ	سَأَلَ
He submitted / accepted Islam.	He worshipped.	He asked.

B : Definitions:

1.) تَاكِيد -stress or emphasis.
2.) مُسْتَقْبِل -future tense verb e.g. يَسْأَلُ He will ask (in future).

C : Conjugation: بحث: نفيِ ب"لَنْ" درْ فِعل مُستقبِل مَعرُوف

He will never do	وَاحِدْ مُذَكَّرْ غَائِبْ	لَنْ يَّفعَلَ
They (2 men) will never do	تَثْنِيَه مُذَكَّرْ غَائِبْ	لَنْ يَّفعَلَا
They (many men) will never do	جَمْعْ مُذَكَّرْ غَائِبْ	لَنْ يَّفعَلُوْا
She will never do	وَاحِدْ مُؤَنَّثْ غَائِبْ	لَنْ تَفعَلَ
They (2 women) will never do	تَثْنِيَه مُؤَنَّثْ غَائِبْ	لَنْ تَفعَلَا
They (many women) will never do	جَمْعْ مُؤَنَّثْ غَائِبْ	لَنْ يَّفعَلْنَ
You (1 man) will never do	وَاحِدْ مُذَكَّرْ حَاضِرْ	لَنْ تَفعَلَ
You (2 men) will vever do	تَثْنِيَه مُذَكَّرْ حَاضِرْ	لَنْ تَفعَلَا
All you men will never do	جَمْعْ مُذَكَّرْ حَاضِرْ	لَنْ تَفعَلُوْا
You (1 woman) will never do	وَاحِدْ مُؤَنَّثْ حَاضِرْ	لَنْ تَفعَلِي
You (2 women) will never do	تَثْنِيَه مُؤَنَّثْ حَاضِرْ	لَنْ تَفعَلَا
All you women will never do	جَمْعْ مُؤَنَّثْ حَاضِرْ	لَنْ تَفعَلْنَ
I will never do	وَاحِدْ مُذَكَّرْ و مُؤَنَّثْ مُتَكَلِّم	لَنْ اَفعَلَ
We will never do	تَثْنِيَه وَجَمْع، مُذَكَّرْ ومُؤَنَّثْ مُتَكَلِّمْ	لَنْ نَفعَلَ

Conjugation: بحث:نَفِی ب"لَن"دَرْ فِعْل مُسْتَقْبِل مَجْهُوْل

He (it) will never be done	وَاحِدْ مُذَكَّرْ غَائِبْ	لَن يُّفعَلَ
They (2 men) will never be done	تَثْنِيَهْ مُذَكَّرْ غَائِبْ	لَن يُّفعَلَا
They (many men) will never be done	جَمْعْ مُذَكَّرْ غَائِبْ	لَن يُّفعَلُوْا
She (it) will nwver be done	وَاحِدْ مُؤَنَّثْ غَائِبْ	لَن تُفعَلَ
They (2 women) will never be done	تَثْنِيَهْ مُؤَنَّثْ غَائِبْ	لَن تُفْعَلَا
They (many women) will never be done	جَمْعْ مُؤَنَّثْ غَائِبْ	لَن يُّفعَلْنَ
You (1 man) will never be done	وَاحِدْ مُذَكَّرْ حَاضِرْ	لَن تُفعَلَ
You (2 men) will never be done	تَثْنِيَهْ مُذَكَّرْ حَاضِرْ	لَن تُفعَلَا
All you men will never be done	جَمْعْ مُذَكَّرْ حَاضِرْ	لَن تُفعَلُوْا
You (1 woman) will never be done	وَاحِدْ مُؤَنَّثْ حَاضِرْ	لَن تُفعَلِي
You (2 women) will never be done	تَثْنِيَهْ مُؤَنَّثْ حَاضِرْ	لَن تُفعَلَا
All you women will never be done	جَمْعْ مُؤَنَّثْ حَاضِرْ	لَن تُفعَلْنَ
I will never be done	وَاحِدْ مُذَكَّرْ و مُؤَنَّثْ مُتَكَلِّم	لَن أُفعَلَ
We will never be done	تَثْنِيَهْ وَجَمْعْ، مُذَكَّرْ وَمُؤَنَّثْ مُتَكَلِّم	لَن نُفعَلَ

Rules of لَنْ **:**

1.) لَنْ is a اَلْحَرْفُ النَّاصِبْ (Al - harf - un nassib). There are four اَلْحُرُوْفُ النَّاصِبَة (Al huroof un naasibah) اِذَنْ (Then), كَيْ (so that, in order), لَنْ (will never) اَنْ (That)

2.) لَنْ appears before a مُضَارِعْ verb and has the following effect:

a.) The five forms which have a dhamma will receive a fatha.

E.g. لَنْ يَّفْعَلَ ، لَنْ تَفْعَلَ ، لَنْ تَفْعَلَ ، لَنْ اَفْعَلَ ، لَنْ نَفْعَلَ

b.) The seven noons following a long vowel (ن اِعْرَابِي) will drop off,
E.g. لَنْ يَّفْعَلَا was يَفْعَلَانِ , ن dropped off

لَنْ يَّفْعَلَا ، لَنْ يَّفْعَلُوْا ، لَنْ تَفْعَلَا ، لَنْ تَفْعَلَا ، لَنْ تَفْعَلُوْا ، لَنْ تَفْعَلِي ، لَنْ تَفْعَلَا

c.) The two feminine plural forms (seghas) will retain their noons i.e. they will not drop off. The reason is that this form is مَبْنِي الْأَصَل , a prime indeclinable word, e.g لَنْ يَّفْعَلْنَ
d.) It will change the meaning of the word to نَفِي تَاكِيْد مُسْتَقْبِل i.e. emphasis of the future negative. In translating we will use the words: will never or will definitely not.

Exercises:

1.) Draw up the "بحث نفی ب"لَنْ conjugation table of the following verbs:

a.) سَأَلَ (مَعْرُوف) b.) مَنَعَ (مَجْهُوْل) With translation

2.) Define:

a.) تَاكِيْد b.) مُسْتَقْبِل

3.) Translate into Arabic:

a.) I will never ask.
b.) I sat on the bed.
c) He is eating fruit.
d.) You (2 men) will never worship idols.
e.) She will never laugh at you.

4.) Translate into English:

a.) لَنْ يَسْمَعَ b.) لَنْ تَجْتَنِبَا c.) لَنْ يَمْنَعْنَ d.) لَنْ تَسْئَلُوْا e.) لَنْ تُغْسَلَا

f.) لَنْ تُضْرَبْنَ g.) لَنْ يَضْحَكَا h.) لَنْ تُفْتَحَ i.) لَنْ تَجْلِسِىْ j.) لَنْ يُتْرَكَا

5.) Identify all the verbs in the following ayaat and write the seghas (mood) and بحث (topic) of each verb:

١) ﴿لَنْ تَنَالُوْا الْبِرَّ حَتّٰى تُنْفِقُوْا مِمَّا تُحِبُّوْنَ﴾(سورة آل عمران: ٩٢)

٢) ﴿لَنْ يَّخْلُقُوْا ذُبَابًا وَّلَوِاجْتَمَعُوْا لَه﴾(سورة الحج: ٧٣)

٣) ﴿لَنْ يَّغْفِرَ اللّٰهُ لَهُمْ﴾(سورة المنافقون: ٦)

٤) ﴿قَالُوْا يَامُوْسٰى اِنَّ فِيْهَا قَوْمًا جَبَّارِيْنَ وَاِنَّا لَنْ نَدْخُلَهَا﴾(سورة المائدة: ٢٢)

٥) ﴿قَالُوْا لَنْ اُرْسِلَهُ مَعَكُمْ حَتّٰى تُؤْتُوْنِ مَوْثِقًا مِّنَ اللّٰهِ﴾ (سورة يوسف: ٦٦)

٦) ﴿قُلْ لَنْ يَّنْفَعَكُمُ الْفِرَارُ اِنْ فَرَرْتُمْ مِنَ الْمَوْتِ﴾(سورة الاحزاب: ١٦)

6.) Write 10 facts in Arabic on any topic of your choice.

LESSON 11
CHAPTER ON THE USAGE OF لَمْ

بَحث نَفِیْ جَحَدْب" لَمْ "

A : Vocabulary:

دَعٰی	رَمٰی	عَلِمَ	نَهٰی
He called.	He threw.	He knew.	He prohibited.

B : Definitions:

1.) نَفِیْ / مَنْفِیْ - Negative i.e. for an action not to occur. e.g. لَمْ يَعْلَمْ He did not know.
2.) حَرْفُ الْعِلَّة - Vowels. In Arabic there are three vowels - ا ، و ، ی

C : Conjugation:

نَفِیْ جَحَدْ ب" لَمْ "مَعْرُوْف

He did not do	وَاحِدْ مُذَكَّرْ غَائِبْ	لَمْ يَفْعَلْ
They (2 men) did not do	تَثْنِيَهْ مُذَكَّرْ غَائِبْ	لَمْ يَفْعَلَا
They (many men) did not do	جَمَعْ مُذَكَّرْ غَائِبْ	لَمْ يَفْعَلُوْا
She did not do	وَاحِدْ مُؤَنَّثْ غَائِبْ	لَمْ تَفْعَلْ
They (two women) did not do	تَثْنِيَهْ مُؤَنَّثْ غَائِبْ	لَمْ تَفْعَلَا
They (many women) did not do	جَمَعْ مُؤَنَّثْ غَائِبْ	لَمْ يَفْعَلْنَ
You (1 man) did not do	وَاحِدْ مُذَكَّرْ حَاضِرْ	لَمْ تَفْعَلْ
You (2 men) did not do	تَثْنِيَهْ مُذَكَّرْ حَاضِرْ	لَمْ تَفْعَلَا
All you men did not do	جَمَعْ مُذَكَّرْ حَاضِرْ	لَمْ تَفْعَلُوْا
You (1 woman) did not do	وَاحِدْ مُؤَنَّثْ حَاضِرْ	لَمْ تَفْعَلِيْ
You (2 women) did not do	تَثْنِيَهْ مُؤَنَّثْ حَاضِرْ	لَمْ تَفْعَلَا
All you women did not do	جَمَعْ مُؤَنَّثْ حَاضِرْ	لَمْ تَفْعَلْنَ
I did not do	وَاحِدْ مُذَكَّرْ و مُؤَنَّثْ مُتَكَلِّمْ	لَمْ اَفْعَلْ
We did not do	تَثْنِيَهْ وَجَمَعْ، مُذَكَّرْ و مُؤَنَّثْ مُتَكَلِّمْ	لَمْ نَفْعَلْ

Conjugation: نَفِيْ جَحَد بلَمْ مَجْهُوْل

He (It) was not done	وَاحِدْ مُذَكَّرْ غَائِبْ	لَمْ يُفْعَلْ
They (2 men) were not done	تَثْنِيَهْ مُذَكَّرْ غَائِبْ	لَمْ يُفْعَلَا
They (many men) were not done	جَمَعْ مُذَكَّرْ غَائِبْ	لَمْ يُفْعَلُوْا
She (It) was not done	وَاحِدْ مُؤَنَّثْ غَائِبْ	لَمْ تُفْعَلْ
They (2 women) were not done	تَثْنِيَهْ مُؤَنَّثْ غَائِبْ	لَمْ تُفْعَلَا
They (many women) were not done	جَمَعْ مُؤَنَّثْ غَائِبْ	لَمْ يُفْعَلْنَ
You (1 man) was not done	وَاحِدْ مُذَكَّرْ حَاضِرْ	لَمْ تُفْعَلْ
You (2 men) were not done	تَثْنِيَهْ مُذَكَّرْ حَاضِرْ	لَمْ تُفْعَلَا
All you men were not done	جَمَعْ مُذَكَّرْ حَاضِرْ	لَمْ تُفْعَلُوْا
You (1 woman) was not done	وَاحِدْ مُؤَنَّثْ حَاضِرْ	لَمْ تُفْعَلِيْ
You (2 women) were not done	تَثْنِيَهْ مُؤَنَّثْ حَاضِرْ	لَمْ تُفْعَلَا
All you women were not done	جَمَعْ مُؤَنَّثْ حَاضِرْ	لَمْ تُفْعَلْنَ
I was not done	وَاحِدْ مُذَكَّرْ و مُؤَنَّثْ مُتَكَلِّمْ	لَمْ أُفْعَلْ
We were not done	تَثْنِيَهْ وَجَمَعْ،مُذَكَّرْومُؤَنَّثْ مُتَكَلِّمْ	لَمْ نُفْعَلْ

Rules:

لَمْ is a اَلْحَرْفُ الْجَازِمْ, There are five اَلْحُرُوفُ الْجَازِمَة,

إِنْ (If), لَمْ (Did not), لَمَّا (Not / when), لِ (Should), لَا (Do not).

لَمْ Comes only before a اَلفِعْلُ الْمُضَارِعْ and has the following effect:

a.) The five forms with a dhamma will receive a sukoon,

E.g.

لَمْ يَفْعَلْ
لَمْ تَفْعَلْ
لَمْ تَفْعَلْ
لَمْ اَفْعَلْ
لَمْ نَفْعَلْ

b.) The seven (ن اِعْرَابِيْ) noons following a long vowel will be deleted:

E.g.

لَمْ يَفْعَلَا
لَمْ تَفْعَلَا
لَمْ تَفْعَلَا

لَمْ تَفْعَلَا

لَمْ يَفْعَلُوْا

لَمْ تَفْعَلُوْا

لَمْ تَفْعَلِيْ

c.) The two noons of جَمع مُؤنَّث will remain intact:

لَمْ يَفْعَلْنَ – لَمْ تَفْعَلْنَ

d.) The حَرْفُ الْعِلَّةُ at the end of a word will drop off:

لَمْ يَرْمِ – يَرْمِىْ

لَمْ يَخْشَ – يَخْشَى

لَمْ يَدْعُ – يَدْعُو

e.) لَمْ Gives a مَاضِىْ مَنْفِىْ (past negative) meaning, i.e. did not, لَمْ يَفْعَلْ He did not do.

D: Exercises

1.) Draw up the conjugations of سَجَدَ and عَلِمَ using لَمْ .

2.) Give the بحث (topic), segha (mood) and translate the following:

a.) لَمْ اَرْمِ b.) لَمْ تدعُوْا c.) لَمْ يَأْكُلْ

d.) لَمْ تُسْجَدِىْ e.) لَمْ تُمْنَعَا g.) لَمْ تُضْحَكْنَ

3.) Translate into Arabic:

a.) I did not eat.
b.) You (1 man) will never eat.
c.) She is being asked.
d.) You many men are not being worshipped.
e.) You (1 woman) did not know.

4.) Choose all the verbs in the following ayaat and write down the mood and topic:

١) ﴿ فَاِنْ لَّمْ تَعْلَمُوْٓا اٰبَآءَهُمْ فَاِخْوَانُكُمْ فِى الدِّيْنِ ﴾ (سورة الاحزاب: ٥)

٢) ﴿ اَلَمْ يَاْتِكُمْ نَذِيْرٌ ﴾ (سورة الملك: ٨)

٣) ﴿ اَلَمْ يَجْعَلْ كَيْدَهُمْ فِىْ تَضْلِيْلٍ ﴾ (سورة الفيل: ٢)

٤) ﴿ اَلَمْ اَقُلْ لَّكَ اِنَّكَ لَنْ تَسْتَطِيْعَ مَعِىَ صَبْرًا ﴾ (سورة الكهف: ٧٢)

٥) ﴿ اَلَمْ اَعْهَدْ اِلَيْكُمْ يٰبَنِىْٓ اٰدَمَ اَنْ لَّا تَعْبُدُوا الشَّيْطٰنَ ﴾ (سورة يٰس: ٦٠)

٦) ﴿ اَفَلَمْ تَكُوْنُوْا تَعْقِلُوْنَ ﴾ (سورة يٰس: ٦٢)

٧) ﴿اَفَلَاتَشْكُرُوْنَ وَاتَّخَذُوْا مِنْ دُوْنِ اللهِ اٰلِهَةً لَعَلَّهُمْ يُنْصَرُوْنَ﴾ (سورة يٰس: ٧٤)

٨) ﴿فَلَا يَحْزُنْكَ قَوْلُهُمْ اِنَّا نَعْلَمُ مَا يُسِرُّوْنَ وَمَايُعْلِنُوْنَ﴾ (سورة يٰس: ٧٦)

5.) Identify all the verbs in the following sentences and write the mood and topic:

١) لَنْ تَبْلُغَ الْمَجْدَ حَتّٰى تَلْعَقَ الصَّبْرَ

٢) مَنْ لَمْ يَشْكُرِ النَّاسَ لَمْ يَشْكُرِ اللهَ

٣) لِمَ لَا تَشْرَبُ اللَّبَنَ كَيْ يَنْفَعَكَ

٤) كَانَ سَعِيْدٌ يَقْرَعُ الْبَابَ فَفَتَحْتُ الْبَابَ لِيَدْخُلَ عَلَيْنَا

٥) اَذِنْتُ لَهُ لِئَلَّا يَحْزَنْ

٦) إِنْ لَمْ تَبْذُلْ جُهْدَكَ لَمْ تَنْجَحْ يَوْمَ الْاِمْتِحَانِ

٧) إِنْ لَمْ تَكْسِلْ تَنْدِمْ

٨) أَمَرْتُ خَادِمِيْ أَنْ لَّا يَخْرُجَ مِنَ الْبَيْتِ حَتّٰى أَرْجِعَ مِنَ الْمَدْرَسَةِ

٩) كُنَّا جَائِعُوْنَ فَاَكَلْنَا الْعِنَبَ حَتّٰى شَبِعْنَا

١٠) إِنْ تَذْهَبْ اِلٰى حَدِيْقَةِ الْحَيَوَانَاتِ تَنْظُرْ عَجَائِبَ خَلْقِ اللهِ مِنَ الْوُحُوْشِ وَالسِّبَاعِ وَالطُّيُوْرِ

١١) قَالَ لِيْ يُوْسُفُ: إِنْ بَذَلْتُ تَمَامَ جُهْدِيْ لَأَنْجَحَ. قُلْتُ لَهُ: اِذَنْ تَبْلُغَ مَرَامَكَ

١٢) إِنْ لَمْ يَكُنْ وِفَاقٌ فَفِرَاقٌ

١٣) اَلَمْ تَقْرَأْ هٰذَا الْكِتَابَ لِتَفْهَمَ الْعَرَبِيَّ

١٤) لَا يَحْزُنُنِيْ إِنْ لَمْ اَبْلُغْ مَرَامِىْ فِيْ أَوَّلِ وَهْلَةٍ بَلْ لَنْ اَتْرُكَ السَّعْىَ حَتّٰى اَبْلُغَ اِلَيْهِ

And from the Qur`aan

١) ﴿فَاِنْ لَّمْ تَفْعَلُوْا وَلَنْ تَفْعَلُوْا فَاتَّقُوْا النَّارَ﴾ (سورة البقرة: ٢٤)

٢) ﴿فَلَنْ اَبْرَحَ الْاَرْضَ حَتّٰى يَأْذَنَ لِيْ أَبِيْ أَوْ يَحْكُمَ اللهُ لِيْ وَ هُوَخَيْرُ الْحَاكِمِيْنَ﴾ (سورة يوسف: ٨٠)

٣) ﴿وَاِذْقَالَ مُوْسٰى لِقَوْمِهِ اِنَّ اللهَ يَاْمُرُكُمْ اَنْ تَذْبَحُوْا بَقَرَةً﴾ (سورة البقرة: ٦٧)

٤) ﴿ اَعُوْذُ بِاللهِ اَنْ اَكُوْنَ مِنَ الْجَاهِلِيْنَ ﴾ (سورة البقرة: ٦٧)

٥) ﴿ اُمِرْتُ اَنْ اَعْبُدَ اللهَ مُخْلِصًا لَّهُ الدِّيْنَ ﴾ (سورة الزمر: ١١)

٦) ﴿ لَئِنْ بَسَطْتَ اِلَيَّ يَدَكَ لِتَقْتُلَنِيْ مَا اَنَا بِبَاسِطٍ يَّدِيَ اِلَيْكَ لِاَقْتُلَكَ ﴾ (سورة المائدة: ٢٨)

٧) ﴿ وَلَمَّا يَدْخُلِ الْاِيْمَانُ فِيْ قُلُوْبِكُمْ ﴾ (سورة الحجرات: ١٤)

٨) ﴿ فَعَلِمَ مَالَمْ تَعْلَمُوْا ﴾ (سورة الفتح: ٢٧)

٩) ﴿ اَلَمْ تَكُنْ اَرْضُ اللهِ وَاسِعَةً ﴾ (سورة النساء: ٩٧)

١٠) ﴿ اَلَمْ تَعْلَمْ اَنَّ اللهَ عَلٰى كُلِّ شَيْءٍ قَدِيْرٌ ﴾ (سورة البقرة: ١٠٦)

١١) ﴿ اِنْ تَنْصُرُوْا اللهَ يَنْصُرْكُمْ ﴾ (سورة محمد: ٧)

LESSON 12

CHAPTER ON THE IMPERATIVE (POSITIVE COMMAD)

بحث اَمْرْ مَعْرُوفْ وَمَجْهُوْلْ

A : Vocabulary:

تَبَسَّمَ	سَجَنَ	رَكَعَ	ظَلَمَ
He smiled.	He imprisoned.	He bowed down.	He oppressed.

B : Definitions:

a) اَمْرْ : Is such a word by means of which a command is given e.g. اِضْرِبْ Hit!, اِرْكَعْ Bow down!

b.) هَمْزَةُ الْوَصْلِ : Is a temporary hamza. It is written but not read when joined to another word, وَقَالَ ارْكَبُوْا However, when found at the beginning of a statment it will be articulated, e.g. اِرْكَبْ

C : Conjugation:

He should do	وَاحِدْ مُذَكَّرْ غَائِبْ	لِيَفْعَلْ
They (2 men) should do	تَثْنِيَهْ مُذَكَّرْ غَائِبْ	لِيَفْعَلَا
They (all men) should do	جَمْعْ مُذَكَّرْ غَائِبْ	لِيَفْعَلُوْا
She should do	وَاحِدْ مُؤَنَّثْ غَائِبْ	لِتَفْعَلْ
They (2 women) should do	تَثْنِيَهْ مُؤَنَّثْ غَائِبْ	لِتَفْعَلَا
They (many women) should do	جَمْعْ مُؤَنَّثْ غَائِبْ	لِيَفْعَلْنَ
Do! (You 1 man)	وَاحِدْ مُذَكَّرْ حَاضِرْ	اِفْعَلْ
You two men do!	تَثْنِيَهْ مُذَكَّرْ حَاضِرْ	اِفْعَلَا
All you men do!	جَمْعْ مُذَكَّرْ حَاضِرْ	اِفْعَلُوْا
Do! (You 1 woman)	وَاحِدْ مُؤَنَّثْ حَاضِرْ	اِفْعَلِيْ
You two women do!	تَثْنِيَهْ مُؤَنَّثْ حَاضِرْ	اِفْعَلَا
All you women do!	جَمْعْ مُؤَنَّثْ حَاضِرْ	اِفْعَلْنَ
I should do	وَاحِدْ مُذَكَّرْ و مُؤَنَّثْ مُتَكَلِّمْ	لِأَفْعَلْ
We should do	تَثْنِيَهْ وَجَمَعْ،مُذَكَّرْوَمُؤَنَّثْ مُتَكَلِّمْ	لِنَفْعَلْ

اَمَرْ is divided into two types:

1.) اَمَرْحَاضِرْ - اَمَرْحَاضِرْ will be made from مُضَارِع حَاضِرْ

2.) اَمَرْغَائِبْ وَ مُتَكَلِّمْ - اَمَرْ غَائِبْ will be made from مَضَارِعْ غَائِب and اَمَرْمُتَكَلِّمْ will be made from مَضَارِعْ مُتَكَلِّمْ

The Rules of Making اَمَرْغَائِبْ and مُتَكَلِّمْ :

1.) Place a Laamul - Amr before the مُضَارِعْ مَعْرُوْف seghas of غَائِب and مُتَكَلِّمْ.

E.g. لِيَفْعَلْ لِاَفْعَلْ

2.) The seghas which have a dhamma will receive a sukoon:

E.g. لِيَفْعَلْ لِتَفْعَلْ لِاَفْعَلْ لِنَفْعَلْ

3.) The ن اِعْرَابِىْ will be deleted:

E.g
لِيَفْعَلَانِ ➡ لِيَفْعَلَا
لِيَفْعَلُوْنَ ➡ لِيَفْعَلُوْا
لِتَفْعَلَانِ ➡ لِتَفْعَلَا

4.) The noon - dhameer will remain intact, e.g. لِيَفْعَلْنَ

5.) The حَرْفُ الْعِلَّة at the end of a word will be dropped off,

e.g. يَدْعُوْ becomes لِيَدْعُ يَرْمِىْ becomes لِيَرْمِ يَخْشَى becomes لِيَخْشَ

6.) Laamul - Amr gives the meaning of 'should', e.g. لِيَفْعَلْ He should do,

لِاَنْصُرْ - I should help لِتَضْرِبْ - She should hit.

7.) اَمَرْ مَجْهُوْل Will be made in the same manner as اَمَرْ مَعْرُوْف ,

e.g. لِيُفْعَلْ He (it) should be done.

The Rules of Making اَمَرْحَاضِرْ :

اَمَرْحَاضِرْ Is made from مُضَارِعْ حَاضِرْ in the following manner:

1.) Delete the عَلَامَةُ الْمُضَارِعْ i.e. The ت

e.g.
تُصَرِّفُ ➡ صَرِّفُ
تَفْعَلُ ➡ فْعَلُ
تَنْصُرُ ➡ نْصُرُ

2.) A.) If the second letter has a saakin then add a هَمْزَةُ الْوَصْلُ . The هَمْزَةُ الْوَصْلُ will receive a dhamma if the عَيْن كَلِمَة (middle radical) has a dhamma.

E.g. أُنْصُرْ Help! أُقْتُلْ Kill!

أُسْجُدْ Prevent! أُعْبُدْ Worship!

The هَمْزَةُ الْوَصْلِ will receive a kasra if the عَيْن كَلِمَة has a kasra or fatha.

E.g اِفْتَحْ Open! اِضْحَكْ Laugh! اِضْرِبْ Hit!

اِمْنَعْ Prevent! اِجْلِسْ Sit!

B.) If the second letter has a harkat then there will be no need to add a هَمْزَةُ الْوَصْلِ

E.g. صَرِّفْ from تُصَرِّفُ Turn!

تَبَسَّمُ from تَتَبَسَّمُ Smile!

عِدُ From تَعِدُ Promise!

دَحْرِجُ from تُدَحْرِجُ Roll!

3.) Thereafter, i) give the last letter a saakin if it has a dhamma. صَرِّفْ

ii) drop off the ن اعرابى صَرِّفِيْ , صَرِّفَا , صَرِّفُوْا

iii) leave the noon dhameer intact, دَحْرِجْنَ , صَرِّفْنَ , اِفْتَحْنَ

iv) drop off the حَرْفُ الْعِلَّة which appears at end of a word. (i.e. if the لَام كَلِمَة has an ا , و or. ى)

أُدْعُ ← أُدْعُو Call / Invite!

اِرْمِ ← اِرْمِى Throw!

اِخْشَ ← اِخْشَى Fear!

The paradigm will be:

Call / Invite! (You 1 man)	وَاحِدْ مُذَكَّرْ حَاضِرْ	أُدْعُ
You two men call / invite!	تَثْنِيَهْ مُذَكَّرْ حَاضِرْ	أُدْعُوَا
All you men call / invite	جَمْعْ مُذَكَّرْ حَاضِرْ	أُدْعُوْا
Call / Invite! (You 1 woman)	وَاحِدْ مُؤَنَّثْ حَاضِرْ	أُدْعِيْ
You two women call / invite!	تَثْنِيَهْ مُؤَنَّثْ حَاضِرْ	أُدْعُوَا
All you women call / invite!	جَمْعْ مُؤَنَّثْ حَاضِرْ	أُدْعِيْنَ

C: Conjugation: بحث اَمَرْ مَجْهُوْل

He should be done	وَاحِدْ مُذَكَّرْ غَائِبْ	لِيُفْعَلْ
They (2 men) should be done	تَثْنِيَهْ مُذَكَّرْ غَائِبْ	لِيُفْعَلَا

They (many men) should be done	جَمْع مُذَكَّرْ غَائِبْ	لِيُفْعَلُوْا
She should be done	وَاحِدْ مُؤَنَّثْ غَائِبْ	لِتُفْعَلْ
They (2 women) should be done	تَثْنِيَه مُؤَنَّثْ غَائِبْ	لِتُفْعَلَا
They (many women) should be done	جَمْع مُؤَنَّثْ غَائِبْ	لِيُفْعَلْنَ
You (1 man) should be done	وَاحِدْ مُذَكَّرْ حَاضِرْ	لِتُفْعَلْ
You (2 men) should be done	تَثْنِيَه مُذَكَّرْ حَاضِرْ	لِتُفْعَلَا
All you men should be done	جَمْع مُذَكَّرْ حَاضِرْ	لِتُفْعَلُوْ
You (1 woman) should be done	وَاحِدْ مُؤَنَّثْ حَاضِرْ	لِتُفْعَلِيْ
You (2 women) should be done	تَثْنِيَه مُؤَنَّثْ حَاضِرْ	لِتُفْعَلَا
All you women should be done	جَمْع مُؤَنَّثْ حَاضِرْ	لِتُفْعَلْنَ
I should be done	وَاحِدْ مُذَكَّرْ و مُؤَنَّثْ مُتَكَلِّمْ	لِأُفْعَلْ
We should be done	تَثْنِيَه وَجَمْع، مُذَكَّرْوَمُؤَنَّثْ مُتَكَلِّمْ	لِنُفْعَلْ

D: Exercise

1.) Draw up the conjugation table of the imperative (اَمرْ) using the following words :

a) ظَلَمَ b) تَبَسَّمَ c) رَمَى d) رَكَعَ

2.) Translate into Arabic:

a.) You (2 men) eat!
b.) All you men drink!
c.) You (1 woman) write!
d.) All those women should hit!
e.) I should hear!
f.) You (2 men) leave!
g.) They (2 women) should go!
h.) They (many men) should prostrate!
i.) You (2 men) ask!
j.) You (many women) refrain!
k.) You (many men) smile!
l.) You (1 woman) turn!
m.) She (1 woman) should prepare!
n.) They (2 men) should carry!

3.) Translate into English:

1.) Draw up the conjugation table of the imperative (اَمرْ) using the following words :

a.) اُقْتُلْ b.) اِجْلِسْنَ c.) اِمْنَعَا d.) اُدْعُوَا e.) لِتَسْأَلَا

f.) لِتَخْشَ g.) لِاَحْتَمِلْ h.) لِأُصَرِّفْ i.) لِنَجْتَنِبْ j.) لِتَظْلِمَا

LESSON 13
CHAPTER ON THE NEGATIVE COMMAND (PROHIBITIVE)

بحث: نہی مَعْرُوْف وَمَجْهُوْل

A : Vocabulary:

خَادَعَ	فَصَلَ	دَخَلَ
He deceived.	He separated	He entered.

B : Definitions :

1.) نَهِي : refers to a command that is negative, e.g لَاتَسْمَعْ - Do not listen! لَاتَلْعَبْ - Do not play!

C: Conjugation:

بحث: نہی مَعْرُوْف

He should not do	وَاحِدْ مُذَكَّرْ غَائِبْ	لَايَفْعَلْ
They (2 men) should not do	تَثْنِيَهْ مُذَكَّرْ غَائِبْ	لَايَفْعَلَا
They (many men) should not do	جَمْعْ مُذَكَّرْ غَائِبْ	لَايَفْعَلُوْا
She should not do	وَاحِدْ مُؤَنَّثْ غَائِبْ	لِاتَفْعَلْ
They (2 women) should not do	تَثْنِيَهْ مُؤَنَّثْ غَائِبْ	لَاتَفْعَلَا
They (many women) should not do	جَمْعْ مُؤَنَّثْ غَائِبْ	لَايَفْعَلْنَ
You (1 man) do not do!	وَاحِدْ مُذَكَّرْ حَاضِرْ	لَاتَفْعَلْ
You (2 men) do not do!	تَثْنِيَهْ مُذَكَّرْ حَاضِرْ	لَاتَفْعَلَا
All you (men) do not do!	جَمْعْ مُذَكَّرْ حَاضِرْ	لَاتَفْعَلُوْا
You (1 woman) do not do!	وَاحِدْ مُؤَنَّثْ حَاضِرْ	لَاتَفْعَلِي
You (2 women) do not do!	تَثْنِيَهْ مُؤَنَّثْ حَاضِرْ	لَاتَفْعَلَا
All (you women) do not do!	جَمْعْ مُؤَنَّثْ حَاضِرْ	لَاتَفْعَلْنَ
I should not do	وَاحِدْ مُذَكَّرْ و مُؤَنَّثْ مُتَكَلِّمْ	لَاأَفْعَلْ
We should not do	تَثْنِيَهْ وَجَمْعْ، مُذَكَّرْوَمُؤَنَّثْ مُتَكَلِّمْ	لَانَفْعَلْ

Rules of making مُضَارِعْ into نَهِي :

a.) Firstly add the particle لَا at the beginning of each segha.
b.) Give the five seghas with a dhamma a sukoon.

لَايَفْعَلْ

لَاتَفْعَلْ

لَاتَفْعَلْ

لَا اَفْعَلْ

لَانَفْعَلْ

c.) The seven اِعْرَابِی " ن " (noons following a long vowel) will drop off.

لَا يَفْعَلَا

لَاتَفْعَلَا x 3

لَاتَفْعَلُوْا

لَاتَفْعَلِيْ

d.) The two noon dhameers will remain intact.

لَاتَفْعَلْنَ - لَايَفْعَلْنَ

e.) The حَرْفُ الْعِلَّة at the end of the word will drop off.

يَرْمِیْ ← لَايَرْمِ

تَدْعُوْ ← لَاتَدْعُ

اَخْشٰی ← لَااَخْشَ

بحث: نَہی مَجْهُوْل

He should not be done	وَاحِدْ مُذَكَّرْ غَائِبْ	لا يُفْعَلْ
They (2 men) should not be done	تَثْنِيَهْ مُذَكَّرْ غَائِبْ	لا يُفْعَلَا
They (many men) should not be done	جَمْعْ مُذَكَّرْ غَائِبْ	لا يُفْعَلُوْا
She should not be done	وَاحِدْ مُؤَنَّثْ غَائِبْ	لا تُفْعَلْ
They (2 women) should not be done	تَثْنِيَهْ مُؤَنَّثْ غَائِبْ	لا تُفْعَلَا
They (many women) should not be done	جَمْعْ مُؤَنَّثْ غَائِبْ	لا يُفْعَلْنَ
You do not be done (man)!	وَاحِدْ مُذَكَّرْ حَاضِرْ	لا تُفْعَلْ
You 2 do not be done (men)!	تَثْنِيَهْ مُذَكَّرْ حَاضِرْ	لا تُفْعَلَا
All do not be done (men)!	جَمْعْ مُذَكَّرْ حَاضِرْ	لا تُفْعَلُوْا
You (1 woman) do not done!	وَاحِدْ مُؤَنَّثْ حَاضِرْ	لا تُفْعَلِيْ
You (2 women) do not be done!	تَثْنِيَهْ مُؤَنَّثْ حَاضِرْ	لا تُفْعَلَا
All (you women) do not be done!	جَمْعْ مُؤَنَّثْ حَاضِرْ	لا تُفْعَلْنَ
I should not be done	وَاحِدْ مُذَكَّرْ و مُؤَنَّثْ مُتَكَلِّمْ	لا أُفْعَلْ
We should not be done	تَثْنِيَهْ وجَمْعْ مُذَكَّرْ مُؤَنَّثْ مُتَكَلِّمْ	لا نُفْعَلْ

D: Exercises:

1) Identify the verbs in the following sentences and then mention its topic and segha:

١) يَا اَحْمَدُ! اِجْلِسْ عَلَى الْكُرْسِيِّ	
٢) اِشْرَبْ الشَّایَ اِنْ لَمْ يَكُنْ لَكَ حَرَجٌ	لَا بَأْسَ فِيْهِ لٰكِنَّ الْآنَ شَرِبْتُ فِي الْبَيْتِ
٣) فَاشْرَبْ الْقَهْوَةَ اِنْ كَانَ لَكَ رَغْبَةٌ فِيْهَا	نَعَمْ يَاسَيِّدِیْ سَمِعْتُ اَنَّ فِنْجَانَ الْقَهْوَةِ بَعْدَ الطَّعَامِ يَنْفَعُ الْهَضْمَ
٤) لٰكِنْ لَاتَشْرَبْ اِلَّا عَلَى اَوْقَاتٍ مُعَيَّنَةٍ	اَحْسَنْتَ يَا سَيِّدِیْ هٰكَذَا اَفْعَلُ
٥) يَا اَحْمَدُ! اِقْرَأْ شَيْئًا مِنَ الْقُرْاٰنِ لِاَسْمَعَ قِرَائَتَكَ	اَنَا أَقْرَأُ آخِرَ سُوْرَةِ الْبَقَرَةِ
٦) هُوَ الطَّبَاشِيْرُ اُكْتُبُوا بِهٖ	مَنْ يَكْتُبُ مِنَّا اَوَّلًا
٧) لِيَكْتُبْ حَامِدٌ اَوَّلاً	اَنَا حَامِدٌ مَا ذَا اَكْتُبُ يَا سَيِّدِیْ
٨) اُكْتُبْ لَايُشْرَبُ اللَّبَنُ عَلَى السَّمَكِ	اُنْظُرْ يَا سَيِّدِیْ هَلْ هٰذَا صَحِيْحٌ

2) Identify the verbs in the following sentences and then mention its topic and segha:

١) ﴿ يَاَيُّهَا النَّاسُ اعْبُدُوْا رَبَّكُمُ الَّذِیْ خَلَقَكُمْ ﴾ (سورة البقرة: ٢١)

٢) ﴿ قَالَ اِبْرَاهِيْمُ رَبِّ اجْعَلْ هٰذَا الْبَلَدَ اٰمِنًا وَّارْزُقْ اَهْلَهٗ مِنَ الثَّمَرَاتِ ﴾ (سورة البقرة: ١٢٦)

٣) ﴿ يَامَرْيَمُ اقْنُتِیْ لِرَبِّكِ وَاسْجُدِیْ وَارْكَعِیْ مَعَ الرَّاكِعِيْنَ ﴾ (سورة آل عمران: ٤٢)

٤) ﴿ فَلْيَعْمَلْ عَمَلًا صَالِحًا ﴾ (سورة الكهف: ١١٠)

٥) ﴿ اِذْهَبْ بِكِتَابِیْ هٰذَا ﴾ (سورة النمل: ٢٨)

٦) ﴿ يَا اَيَّتُهَا النَّفْسُ الْمُطْمَئِنَّةُ ارْجِعِیْ اِلٰى رَبِّكِ رَاضِيَةً مَرْضِيَّةً ﴾ (سورة الفجر: ٢٧، ٢٨)

٧) ﴿ يٰبَنِیَّ لَاتَدْخُلُوْا مِنْ بَابٍ وَّاحِدٍ وَادْخُلُوْا مِنْ اَبْوَابٍ مُتَفَرِّقَةٍ ﴾ (سورة يوسف: ٦٧)

٨) ﴿ لَاتَحْزَنْ اِنَّ اللّٰهَ مَعَنَا ﴾ (سورة التوبة: ٤٠)

٩) ﴿ لَايَحْزُنْكَ قَوْلُهُمْ ﴾

١٠) ﴿ وَلَاتَحْسَبَنَّ اللّٰهَ غَافِلًا عَمَّا يَعْمَلُ الظَّالِمُوْنَ ﴾ (سورة ابراهيم: ٤٢)

١١) ﴿ لَاتَحْسَبَنَّ الَّذِيْنَ قُتِلُوْا فِیْ سَبِيْلِ اللّٰهِ اَمْوَاتًا بَلْ اَحْيَاءٌ عِنْدَرَبِّهِمْ يُرْزَقُوْنَ ﴾ (سورة آل عمران: ١٦٩)

١٣) ﴿ وَلَاتَقْرَبُوْا الْفَوَاحِشَ ﴾ (سورة الانعام: ١٥١)

١٢) ﴿ كُوْنُوْا قَوَّامِيْنَ بِالْقِسْطِ ﴾ (سورة النساء: ١٣٥)

١٤) ﴿ لَايَسْخَرْ قَوْمٌ مِنْ قَوْمٍ عَسَى اَنْ يَكُوْنُوْا خَيْراً مِنْهُمْ ﴾ (سورة الحجرات: ١١)

١٥) ﴿ إِنَّمَا الْمُشْرِكُوْنَ نَجَسٌ فَلَا يَقْرَبُوا الْمَسْجِدَ الْحَرَامَ بَعْدَ عَامِهِمْ هٰذَا ﴾ (سورة التوبة: ٢٨)

١٦) ﴿ وَإِذَا قُلْتُمْ فَاعْدِلُوْا وَلَوْ كَانَ ذَا قُرْبٰى ﴾ (سورة الانعام: ١٥٢)

١٧) ﴿ وَلَا تَأْكُلُوْا مِمَّا لَمْ يُذْكَرِ اسْمُ اللهِ ﴾ (سورة الانعام: ١٢١)

3.) Place the correct i'raab on the following passage:

انظر يا خالد! إلى كتابك واقرأ درسك ولاتنظر إلى يمينك والى يسارك وإن لم تفهم فاسئل استاذك،ولما فرغت من الدرس فاذهب إلى بيتك ولاتلعب مع الأولاد فى الطريق واحفظ دروسك بعد صلاة المغرب،واكتب واجبات المدرسة ولاتكن من الغافلين

LESSON 14
CHAPTER ON THE POSITIVE EMPHATIC FORM

لام تاکید بَا نُون تاکِید ثَقِیْلہ و خَفِیْفہ دَرْ فعل مُسْتَقْبِل مَعْرُوْف وَ مَجْهُوْل

A : Vocabulary:

اَخَذَ	ذَكَرَ
He took.	He remembered

The emphatic noon (ن تاکید) is of two types:

1. ن ثَقِیْلَہ - نَّ i.e. a noon with a tasheed.
2. ن خَفِیْفَہ - نْ i.e. a noon with a sukoon.

ن ثَقِیْلَہ appears in all 14 seghas while ن خَفِیْفَہ appears in only eight. It does not appear in the six forms which have an alif before the ن اعرابی . The emphatic laam (لام تاکید) is always مَفْتُوْح.

ثقیلہ معروف

He will definitely do	وَاحِدْ مُذَكَّرْ غَائِبْ	لَيَفْعَلَنَّ
They (2 men) will definitely do	تَثْنِيَهْ مُذَكَّرْ غَائِبْ	لَيَفْعَلَانِّ
They (many men) will definitely do	جَمْعْ مُذَكَّرْ غَائِبْ	لَيَفْعَلُنَّ
She will definitely do	وَاحِدْ مُؤَنَّثْ غَائِبْ	لَتَفْعَلَنَّ
They (2 women) will definitely do	تَثْنِيَهْ مُؤَنَّثْ غَائِبْ	لَتَفْعَلَانِّ
They (many women) will definitely do	جَمْعْ مُؤَنَّثْ غَائِبْ	لَيَفْعَلْنَانِّ
You (1 man) will definitely do	وَاحِدْ مُذَكَّرْ حَاضِرْ	لَتَفْعَلَنَّ
You (2 men) will definitely do	تَثْنِيَهْ مُذَكَّرْ حَاضِرْ	لَتَفْعَلَانِّ
All you men will definitely do	جَمْعْ مُذَكَّرْ حَاضِرْ	لَتَفْعَلُنَّ
You (1 woman) will definitely do	وَاحِدْ مُؤَنَّثْ حَاضِرْ	لَتَفْعَلِنَّ
You (2 women) will definitely do	تَثْنِيَهْ مُؤَنَّثْ حَاضِرْ	لَتَفْعَلَانِّ
All you women will definitely do	جَمْعْ مُؤَنَّثْ حَاضِرْ	لَتَفْعَلْنَانِّ
I will definitely do	وَاحِدْ مُذَكَّرْ و مُؤَنَّثْ مُتَكَلِّمْ	لَاَفْعَلَنَّ
We will definitely do	تَثْنِيَهْ وجَمْعْ مُذَكَّرْ مُؤَنَّثْ مُتَكَلِّمْ	لَنَفْعَلَنَّ

ثقیلہ مجہول

He (it) will definitely be done	وَاحِدْ مُذَکَّرْ غَائِبْ	لَيُفْعَلَنَّ
They (2 men) will definitely be done	تَثْنِيَهْ مُذَکَّرْ غَائِبْ	لَيُفْعَلَانِّ
They (many men) will definitely be done	جَمْعْ مُذَکَّرْ غَائِبْ	لَيُفْعَلُنَّ
She (it) will definitely be done	وَاحِدْ مُؤَنَّثْ غَائِبْ	لَتُفْعَلَنَّ
They (2 women) will definitely be done	تَثْنِيَهْ مُؤَنَّثْ غَائِبْ	لَتُفْعَلَانِّ
They (many women) will definitely be done	جَمْعْ مُؤَنَّثْ غَائِبْ	لَيُفْعَلْنَانِّ
You (1 man) will definitely be done	وَاحِدْ مُذَکَّرْ حَاضِرْ	لَتُفْعَلَنَّ
You (2 men) will definitely be done	تَثْنِيَهْ مُذَکَّرْ حَاضِرْ	لَتُفْعَلَانِّ
All you men will definitely be done	جَمْعْ مُذَکَّرْ حَاضِرْ	لَتُفْعَلُنَّ
You (1 woman) will definitely be done	وَاحِدْ مُؤَنَّثْ حَاضِرْ	لَتُفْعَلِنَّ
You (2 woman) will definitely be done	تَثْنِيَهْ مُؤَنَّثْ حَاضِرْ	لَتُفْعَلَانِّ
All you women will definitely be done	جَمْعْ مُؤَنَّثْ حَاضِرْ	لَتُفْعَلْنَانِّ
I will definitely be done	وَاحِدْ مُذَکَّرْ و مُؤَنَّثْ مُتَکَلِّمْ	لَأُفْعَلَنَّ
We will definitely be done	تَثْنِيَهْ وَجَمْعْ مُذَکَّرْوَمُؤَنَّثْ مُتَکَلِّمْ	لَنُفْعَلَنَّ

خفیفہ معروف

He will definitely do	وَاحِدْ مُذَکَّرْ غَائِبْ	لَيَفْعَلَنْ
They (many men) will definitely do	جَمْعْ مُذَکَّرْ غَائِبْ	لَيَفْعَلُنْ
She will definitely do	وَاحِدْ مُؤَنَّثْ غَائِبْ	لَتَفْعَلَنْ
You (1 man) will definitely do	وَاحِدْ مُذَکَّرْ حَاضِرْ	لَتَفْعَلَنْ
All you men will definitely do	جَمْعْ مُذَکَّرْ حَاضِرْ	لَتَفْعَلُنْ
You (1 woman) will definitely do	وَاحِدْ مُؤَنَّثْ حَاضِرْ	لَتَفْعَلِنْ
I will definitely do	وَاحِدْ مُذَکَّرْ و مُؤَنَّثْ مُتَکَلِّمْ	لَأَفْعَلَنْ
We will definitely do	تَثْنِيَهْ وَجَمْعْ مُذَکَّرْوَمُؤَنَّثْ مُتَکَلِّمْ	لَنَفْعَلَنْ

خفیفہ مجہول

He (It) will definitely be done	وَاحِدْ مُذَكَّرْ غَائِبْ	لَيُفْعَلَنْ
They (many men) will definitely be done	جَمْعْ مُذَكَّرْ غَائِبْ	لَيُفْعَلُنْ
She (It) will definitely be done	وَاحِدْ مُؤَنَّثْ غَائِبْ	لَتُفْعَلَنْ
You (1 man) will definitely be done	وَاحِدْ مُذَكَّرْ حَاضِرْ	لَتُفْعَلَنْ
All you men will definitely be done	جَمْعْ مُذَكَّرْ حَاضِرْ	لَتُفْعَلُنْ
You (1 woman) will definitely be done	وَاحِدْ مُؤَنَّثْ حَاضِرْ	لَتُفْعَلِنْ
I will definitely be done	وَاحِدْ مُذَكَّرْ و مُؤَنَّثْ مُتَكَلِّمْ	لَأُفْعَلَنْ
We will definitely be done	تَثْنِيَهْ وجَمْعْ مُذَكَّرْ مُؤَنَّثْ مُتَكَلِّمْ	لَنُفْعَلَنْ

The Rules of Making the Emphatic Form:

a.) Add a لام تاکِید i.e. a laam with a fatha at the beginning of مُضَارِعْ .

b.) Add a ن at the end, e.g. لَيَفْعَلَنَّ

c.) The five seghas with a dhamma will receive a fatha.

لَنَفْعَلَنَّ	لَأَفْعَلَنَّ	لَتَفْعَلَنَّ	لَتَفْعَلَنَّ	لَيَفْعَلَنَّ

d.) The seven ن اعرابی will drop off and will be replaced by a ن ثقیلہ .

لَتَفْعَلَانِّ	لَتَفْعَلَانِّ	لَيَفْعَلُنَّ	لَيَفْعَلَانِّ
	لَتَفْعَلَانِّ	لَتَفْعَلِنَّ	لَتَفْعَلُنَّ

e.) The two noon dhameers will remain intact and an الف الفاصل will be added after it. An Alif-ul-Faasil is a separating alif. It separates the noon dhameer (noon of the feminine plural) (ن جَمْعْ مُؤَنَّثْ) and the emphatic noon (ن ثقیلہ).

لَتَفْعَلْنَانِّ	لَيَفْعَلْنَانِّ

F.) The واو of جَمْعْ مُذَكَّرْ غَائِبْ and جَمْعْ مُذَكَّرْ حَاضِرْ will drop off.

لَيَفْعَلُنَّ	لَتَفْعَلُنَّ

F.) The يا of وَاحِدْ مُؤَنَّثْ حَاضِر will drop off.

تَفْعَلِيْنَ	←	لَتَفْعَلِنَّ

I'raab (vowel signs) of the Various Seghas (Forms):

1.) There is an alif before the ن ثقيله in six seghas. They are the four dual forms and the two feminine plural forms.

2.) There is a dhamma before the ن ثقيله in the two masculine plural forms.

3.) There is a kasra before the ن ثقيله in the feminie singular second person.

4.) There is a fatha before the ن ثقيله in all the remaining singular forms and the one جَمْع مُتَكَلِّم segha.

5.) After alif the ن ثقيله is مَكْسُوْر and in the remaining seghas it is مَفْتُوْح .

Note:

1.) ن خفيفه has the same rules as ن ثقيله . The only difference is in the sukoon (khafeefah) and tashdeed (thaqeelah).

2.) ن ثقيله و خفيفه give a future emphatic meaning, i.e. will/shall definitely,

e.g. لَيَفْعَلَنَّ He shall definitely do/ He will definitely do!

3.) Sometimes a لَام تَاكِيْد i.e. لَ is added before مُضَارِع without adding a ن تاكيد . In this case it will restrict مُضَارِع to the present tense. e.g. لَيَكْتُبُ زَيْدٌ Zaid is writing.

D: Exercises:

1) Draw up conjugation tables of لَام تَاكِيد بَانُوْن تَاكِيد ثَقِيْلَه using the following words:

a) أَخَذَ b) أَمَرَ

2) Give the بحث (topic), segha (mood) and translation of the following:

a) لَيَضْرِبُنَّ b) لَتُقْتَلِنَّ c.) لَيَأْخُذَنَّ d.) لَتَدْخُلُنَّ

e.) لَأَسْجُدَنَّ f.) لَنُفْعَلَنَّ g.) لَتُضْحَكَنَّ h.) لَيَعْلَمَانِّ

i.) لَتَلْبَسَانِّ j.) لَتَغْسِلْنَانِّ k.) لَتَأْكُلْنَانِّ l.) لَتَشْرَبَنَّ

3.1.) Identify the verbs which have لَام تَاكِيْد and نُوْنِ تَاكِيْد .

3.2.) Write the بحث (topic) and segha (mood) of each one.

3.3.) Translate each sentence.

١) لَأَكْتُبَنَّ الْيَوْمَ مَكْتُوْبًا اِلَى خَالَتِيْ

٢) لَتَذْهَبَنَّ إِلَى الصَّيْدِ

٣) هٰذَانِ رَجُلَانِ لَيُقْتَلَانِّ لِاَنَّهُمَا قَاتِلَا زَيْدٍ

٤) هٰذَا الْوَلَدُ لَنْ يَقْرَأَ وَلَنْ يَكْتُبَ اَمَّا اُخْتَاهُ تَانِكَ فَلَتَقْرَأَنِّ وَلَتَكْتُبَانِّ

٥) لَيَنْجَحَانِّ اَخَوَاىَ فِيْ هٰذَا الْعَامِ اِنْ شَاءَ اللهُ

And from the Qur'aan:

١) ﴿وَلَيَنْصُرَنَّ اللهُ مَنْ يَّنْصُرُهُ﴾(سورة الحج: ٤٠)

٢) ﴿لَتَدْخُلُنَّ الْمَسْجِدَ الْحَرَامَ اِنْ شَاءَ اللهُ اٰمِنِيْنَ﴾(سورة الفتح: ٢٧)

٣) ﴿رَبَّنَا ظَلَمْنَا اَنْفُسَنَا وَاِنْ لَّمْ تَغْفِرْ لَنَا وَتَرْحَمْنَا لَنَكُوْنَنَّ مِنَ الْخَاسِرِيْنَ﴾(سورة الأعراف: ٢٣)

٤) ﴿لَئِنْ لَّمْ يَفْعَلْ مَا اٰمُرُهُ لَيُسْجَنَنَّ وَلَيَكُوْنًا(لَيَكُوْنَنَّ) مِنَ الصَّاغِرِيْنَ﴾(سورة يوسف: ٣٢)

ن ثَقِيْلَه وخَفِيْفَه is suffixed to the imperative (اَمْرْ) and prohibitive (نَهِى) paradigms as well. thus emphasise the اَمْرْ and نَهِى .

Examples:

He should definitely do	لِيَفْعَلَنَّ
He should definitely be done	لِيُفْعَلَنَّ
He should definitely do	لِيَفْعَلَنْ
He should definitely be done	لِيُفْعَلَنْ
He should definitely not do	لَايَفْعَلَنَّ
He should definitely not be done	لَايُفْعَلَنَّ
He should definitely not do	لَايَفْعَلَنْ
He should definitely not be done	لَايُفْعَلَنْ

بحث امر بانون ثقيله معروف

He should definitely do	وَاحِدْ مُذَكَّرْ غَائِبْ	لِيَفْعَلَنَّ
They (2 men) should definitely do	تَثْنِيَهْ مُذَكَّرْ غَائِبْ	لِيَفْعَلَانِّ
They (many men) should definitely do	جَمْعْ مُذَكَّرْ غَائِبْ	لِيَفْعَلُنَّ
She should definitely do	وَاحِدْ مُؤَنَّثْ غَائِبْ	لِتَفْعَلَنَّ
They (2 women) should definitely do	تَثْنِيَهْ مُؤَنَّثْ غَائِبْ	لِتَفْعَلَانِّ
They (many women) should definitely do	جَمْعْ مُؤَنَّثْ غَائِبْ	لِيَفْعَلْنَانِّ
You (1 man) definitely do!	وَاحِدْ مُذَكَّرْ حَاضِرْ	اِفْعَلَنَّ

You (2 men) definitely do!	تَثْنِیَہْ مُذَکَّرْ حَاضِرْ	اِفْعَـلَانِّ
All you men definitely do!	جَمْعْ مُذَکَّرْ حَاضِرْ	اِفْعَلُنَّ
You (1 woman) definitely do!	وَاحِدْ مُؤنَّثْ حَاضِرْ	اِفْعَلِنَّ
You (2 women) definitely do!	تَثْنِیَہْ مُؤنَّثْ حَاضِرْ	اِفْعَـلَانِّ
All you women definitely do!	جَمْعْ مُؤنَّثْ حَاضِرْ	اِفْعَلْنَانِّ
I should definitely do	وَاحِدْ مُذَکَّرْ و مُؤنَّثْ مُتَکَلِّمْ	لِأَفْعَلَنَّ
We should definitely do	تَثْنِیَہْ وجَمْعْ مُذَکَّرْوَمُؤنَّثْ مُتَکَلِّمْ	لِنَفْعَلَنَّ

بحث امر بانون ثقیلہ مجھول

He should definitely be done	وَاحِدْ مُذَکَّرْ غَائِبْ	لِيُفْعَلَنَّ
They (2 men) should definitely be done	تَثْنِيَہْ مُذَکَّرْ غَائِبْ	لِيُفْعَـلَانِّ
They (many men) should definitely be done	جَمْعْ مُذَکَّرْ غَائِبْ	لِيُفْعَلُنَّ
She should definitely be done	وَاحِدْ مُؤنَّثْ غَائِبْ	لِتُفْعَلَنَّ
They (2 women) should definitely be done	تَثْنِيَہْ مُؤنَّثْ غَائِبْ	لِتُفْعَـلَانِّ
They (many women) should definitely be done	جَمْعْ مُؤنَّثْ غَائِبْ	لِيُفْعَلْنَانِّ
You (1 man) should definitely be done!	وَاحِدْ مُذَکَّرْ حَاضِرْ	لِتُفْعَلَنَّ
You (2 men) should definitely be done!	تَثْنِيَہْ مُذَکَّرْ حَاضِرْ	لِتُفْعَـلَانِّ
All you men should definitely be done!	جَمْعْ مُذَکَّرْ حَاضِرْ	لِتُفْعَلُنَّ
You (1 woman) should definitely be done!	وَاحِدْ مُؤنَّثْ حَاضِرْ	لِتُفْعَلِنَّ
You (2 women) should definitely be done!	تَثْنِيَہْ مُؤنَّثْ حَاضِرْ	لِتُفْعَـلَانِّ
All you women should definitely be done!	جَمْعْ مُؤنَّثْ حَاضِرْ	لِتُفْعَلْنَانِّ
I should definitely be done	وَاحِدْ مُذَکَّرْ وَ مُؤنَّثْ مُتَکَلِّمْ	لِأُفْعَلَنَّ
We shuould definitely be done	تَثْنِيَہْ وجَمْعْ مُذَکَّرْومُؤنَّثْ مُتَکَلِّمْ	لِنُفْعَلَنَّ

بحث امر بانون خفیفہ معروف

He should definitely do	وَاحِدْ مُذَکَّرْ غَائِبْ	لِيَفْعَلَنْ
They (many men) should definitely do	جَمْعْ مُذَکَّرْ غَائِبْ	لِيَفْعَلُنْ
She should definitely do	وَاحِدْ مُؤنَّثْ غَائِبْ	لِتَفْعَلَنْ

You (1 man) definitely do!	وَاحِدْ مُذَكَّرْ حَاضِرْ	اِفْعَلَنْ
All you men definitely do!	جَمْعْ مُذَكَّرْ حَاضِرْ	اِفْعَلُنْ
You (1 woman) definitely do!	وَاحِدْ مُؤَنَّثْ حَاضِرْ	اِفْعَلِنْ
I should definitely do	وَاحِدْ مُذَكَّرْ و مُؤَنَّثْ مُتَكَلِّمْ	لِأَفْعَلَنْ
We should definitely do	تَثْنِيَهْ وجَمْعْ مُذَكَّرْ مُؤَنَّثْ مُتَكَلِّمْ	لِنَفْعَلَنْ

بحث امر بانون خفیفه مجهول

He should definitely be done	وَاحِدْ مُذَكَّرْ غَائِبْ	لِيُفْعَلَنْ
They (many men) should definitely be done	جَمْعْ مُذَكَّرْ غَائِبْ	لِيُفْعَلُنْ
She should definitely be done	وَاحِدْ مُؤَنَّثْ غَائِبْ	لِتُفْعَلَنْ
You (1 man) should definitely be done	وَاحِدْ مُذَكَّرْ حَاضِرْ	لِتُفْعَلَنْ
All you men should definitely be done	جَمْعْ مُذَكَّرْ حَاضِرْ	لِتُفْعَلُنْ
You (1 woman) should definitely be done	وَاحِدْ مُؤَنَّثْ حَاضِرْ	لِتُفْعَلِنْ
I should definitely be done	وَاحِدْ مُذَكَّرْ و مُؤَنَّثْ مُتَكَلِّمْ	لِأُفْعَلَنْ
We should definitely be done	تَثْنِيَهْ وجَمْعْ مُذَكَّرْ مُؤَنَّثْ مُتَكَلِّمْ	لِنُفْعَلَنْ

بحث نهی بانون ثقیله معروف

He should definitely not do	وَاحِدْ مُذَكَّرْ غَائِبْ	لَايَفْعَلَنَّ
They (2 men) should definitely not do	تَثْنِيَهْ مُذَكَّرْ غَائِبْ	لَايَفْعَلَانِّ
They (many men) should definitely not do	جَمْعْ مُذَكَّرْ غَائِبْ	لَايَفْعَلُنَّ
She should definitely not do	وَاحِدْ مُؤَنَّثْ غَائِبْ	لَاتَفْعَلَنَّ

They (2 women) should definitely not do	تَثْنِيَهْ مُؤنَّثْ غَائِبْ	لَاتَفْعَلَانِّ
They (many women) should definitely not do	جَمْعْ مُؤنَّثْ غَائِبْ	لَايَفْعَلْنَانِّ
You (1 man) definitely do not do!	وَاحِدْ مُذَكَّرْ حَاضِرْ	لَاتَفْعَلَنَّ
You (2 men) definitely do not do!	تَثْنِيَهْ مُذَكَّرْ حَاضِرْ	لَاتَفْعَلَانِّ
All you men definitely do not do!	جَمْعْ مُذَكَّرْ حَاضِرْ	لَاتَفْعَلُنَّ
You (1 woman) definitely do not do!	وَاحِدْ مُؤنَّثْ حَاضِرْ	لَاتَفْعَلِنَّ
You (2 women) definitely do not do!	تَثْنِيَهْ مُؤنَّثْ حَاضِرْ	لَاتَفْعَلَانِّ
All you women definitely do not do!	جَمْعْ مُؤنَّثْ حَاضِرْ	لَاتَفْعَلْنَانِّ
I should definitely not do	وَاحِدْ مُذَكَّرْ و مُؤنَّثْ مُتَكَلِّمْ	لَااَفْعَلَنَّ
We shuould definitely not do	تَثْنِيَهْ وجَمْعْ مُذَكَّرْ مُؤنَّثْ مُتَكَلِّمْ	لَانَفْعَلَنَّ

بحث نہی بانون ثقیلہ مجہول

He should definitely not be done	وَاحِدْ مُذَكَّرْ غَائِبْ	لَايُفْعَلَنَّ
They (2 men) should definitely not be done	تَثْنِيَهْ مُذَكَّرْ غَائِبْ	لَايُفْعَلَانِّ
They (many men) should definitely not be done	جَمْعْ مُذَكَّرْ غَائِبْ	لَايُفْعَلُنَّ
She should definitely not be done	وَاحِدْ مُؤنَّثْ غَائِبْ	لَاتُفْعَلَنَّ
They (2 women) should definitely not be done	تَثْنِيَهْ مُؤنَّثْ غَائِبْ	لَاتُفْعَلَانِّ
They (many women) should definitely not be done	جَمْعْ مُؤنَّثْ غَائِبْ	لَايُفْعَلْنَانِّ
You (1 man) should definitely not be done	وَاحِدْ مُذَكَّرْ حَاضِرْ	لَاتُفْعَلَنَّ
You (2 men) should definitely not be done	تَثْنِيَهْ مُذَكَّرْ حَاضِرْ	لَاتُفْعَلَانِّ
All you men should definitely not be done	جَمْعْ مُذَكَّرْ حَاضِرْ	لَاتُفْعَلُنَّ
You (1 woman) should definitely not be done	وَاحِدْ مُؤنَّثْ حَاضِرْ	لَاتُفْعَلِنَّ
You (2 women) should definitely not be done	تَثْنِيَهْ مُؤنَّثْ حَاضِرْ	لَاتُفْعَلَانِّ
All you women should definitely not be done	جَمْعْ مُؤنَّثْ حَاضِرْ	لَاتُفْعَلْنَانِّ
I should definitely not be done	وَاحِدْ مُذَكَّرْ و مُؤنَّثْ مُتَكَلِّمْ	لَااُفْعَلَنَّ
We should definitely not be done	تَثْنِيَهْ وجَمْعْ مُذَكَّرْ مُؤنَّثْ مُتَكَلِّمْ	لَانُفْعَلَنَّ

بحث نہی با نون خفیفہ معروف

He should definitely not do	وَاحِدْ مُذَكَّرْ غَائِبْ	لَايَفْعَلَنْ

They (many men) should definitely not do	جَمْعْ مُذَکَّرْ غَائِبْ	لَايَفْعَلُنْ
She should definitely not do	وَاحِدْ مُؤنَّثْ غَائِبْ	لَاتَفْعَلَنْ
You (1 man) definitely do not do	وَاحِدْ مُذَکَّرْ حَاضِرْ	لَاتَفْعَلَنْ
All you men definitely do not do	جَمْعْ مُذَکَّرْ حَاضِرْ	لَاتَفْعَلُنْ
You (1 woman) definitely do not do	وَاحِدْ مُؤنَّثْ حَاضِرْ	لَاتَفْعَلِنْ
I should definitely not do	وَاحِدْ مُذَکَّرْ وَ مُؤنَّثْ مُتَکَلِّمْ	لَاأَفْعَلَنْ
We should definitely not do	تَثْنِيَهْ وَجَمْعْ مُذَکَّرْوَمُؤنَّثْ مُتَکَلِّمْ	لَانَفْعَلَنْ

بحث نهی با نون خفیفه مجهول

He should definitely not be done	وَاحِدْ مُذَکَّرْ غَائِبْ	لَايُفْعَلَنْ
They (many men) should definitely not be done	جَمْعَ مُذَکَّرْ غَائِبْ	لَايُفْعَلُنْ
She should definitely not be done	وَاحِدْ مُؤنَّثْ غَائِبْ	لَاتُفْعَلَنْ
You (1 man) should definitely not be done	وَاحِدْ مُذَکَّرْ حَاضِرْ	لَاتُفْعَلَنْ
All you men should definitely not be done	جَمْعَ مُذَکَّرْ حَاضِرْ	لَاتُفْعَلُنْ
You (1 woman) should definitely not be done	وَاحِدْ مُؤنَّثْ حَاضِرْ	لَاتُفْعَلِنْ
I should definitely not be done	وَاحِدْ مُذَکَّرْ وَ مُؤنَّثْ مُتَکَلِّمْ	لَااُ ْعَلَنْ
We should definitely not be done	تَثْنِيَهْ وَجَمْعَ مُذَکَّرْوَمُؤنَّثْ مُتَکَلِّمْ	لَانُفْعَلَنْ

E : Exercises:

1.) Draw up the نَهِى **and** اَمَرْ **conjugation tables with** ن ثَقِيْلَه و خَفِيْفَه **using the word** اَخَذَ

2.) Give the بَحث **, segha and translation of the following:**

a.) لَيَسْجُدُنَّ	b.) لَتَقْتُلَنَّ	c.) لَتَقْتُلِنَّ	d.) لَاتَقْتُلِنْ
e.) لَاتَقْتُلِنَّ	f.) لِيَأمُرُنَّ	g.) لِيَرْكَعَنْ	h.) اُقْتُلْنَانِّ
i.) لَاتَضْحَكَانِّ	j.) اُسْجُدُنَّ	k.) اُسْجُدُنْ	l.) اِسْأَلَانِّ
m.) لِيَسْأَلَانِّ	n.) لِيَضْحَكَا	o.) لَاتَمْنَعِنَّ	p.) لَاتَجْلِسَنَّ
q.) لَاتَتْرُكُنَّ	r.) خُذُنْ (اُوْخُذُنْ)	s.) اُذْكُرَانِّ	t.) لِيُسْجَدْنَانِّ

LESSON 15
THE ACTIVE PARTICIPLE

اِسْمُ الْفَاعِل

A : Vocabulary:

قَرَأَ	طَلَبَ	لَعِبَ
He recited.	He sought.	He played.

B : Definitions:

اسم الفاعل :is that noun which explains the doer of the action. It is an ism derived from a مَصْدَر (root word) and has a particular scale. In this aspect it differs from a فَاعِل which does not have to be a derivative noun. The فَاعِل must be with its فِعْل ,while an اِسْمُ الْفَاعِل does not need to accompany a فِعْل or فَاعِل e.g. قَاتِلٌ One male killer. ضَارِبٌ One male who hits.

C: اسم الفاعل Of triliteral words will be placed on the following scale:

	MALE	MEANING	FEMALE	MEANING
SINGULAR	فَاعِلٌ	1 Male doer	فَاعِلَةٌ	1 Female doer
DUAL	فَاعِلَانِ	2 male doers	فَاعِلَتَانِ	2 female doers
PLURAL	فَاعِلُوْنَ	Many male doers	فَاعِلَاتٌ	Many female doers

اسم الفاعل can be used to show the first, second and third person. If one desires, a dhameer (pronoun) may be added to indicate the first, second and third persons.

E.g.		هِيَ فَاعِلَةٌ	هُوَ فَاعِلٌ
	اَنْتِ فَاعِلَةٌ	هُمَا فَاعِلَتَانِ	هُمَا فَاعِلَانِ
		هُنَّ فَاعِلَاتٌ	هُمْ فَاعِلُوْنَ

The active participle of a فِعْل لَازِم (intransitive verb) or مَاضِيْ مَضْمُوْمُ الْعَيْن i.e. those past tense verbs that have a dhamma on the middle radical will be on the scale of the sifat فَعِيْلٌ .

E.g. كَرُمَ will become كَرِيْمٌ

لَطُفَ will become لَطِيْفٌ

قَرُبَ will become قَرِيْبٌ

When اَلْ is prefixed to it, it incorporates all three tenses e.g. اَلْكَرِيْمُ Translation.........who honoured / who honours / who will honour. However, without اَلْ it incorporates only the present and future tense.

The اسم الفاعل of a quadriliteral (four lettered word), or those words that do not have three original letters will be made as follows:

1.) Drop off the عَلَامَةُ الْمُضَارِعْ المَعْرُوْف , i.e. ي - كَرُمَ

2.) Replace it with a اَلْمِيْمُ الْمَضْمُوْم i.e. مُ - مُكْرِمُ

3.) Give the عَيْن كَلِمَه (middle radical / second last letter) a kasra if it does not already have one.

مُجْتَنِبُ مُكْرِمُ

4.) Give the last letter a tanween مُتَبَسِّمٌ مُكْرِمٌ مُجْتَنِبٌ

D: Exercises:

1.) Draw up the اسم الفاعل conjugation tables of the following words :

a.) لَعِبَ b.) طَلَبَ c.) يُدَحْرِجُ d.) يَتَسَرْبَلُ e.) قَرَأَ

2.) Change the following words into singular masculine forms of اسم الفاعل .

a.) All the words listed in your vocabulary thus far.

b.) يُعْلِنُ c.) يُحَرِّمُ d.) يَتَبَاعَدُ e.) يُخَادِعُ f.) يُقَاتِلُ

g.) يُقَنْطِرُ h.) يَحْرَنْجِمُ i.) يَتَبَخْتَرُ J.) يَنْفَطِرُ k.) يَنْشَعِبُ

l.) يَدْهَامُّ m.) يَجْلَوِّذُ n.) يُسْلِمُ

3.) Identify the active participle in the following ayaat. Mention the mood and بحث (topic) as well:

١) ﴿ تَوَفَّنِيْ مُسْلِمًا وَاَلْحِقْنِيْ بِالصَّالِحِيْنَ ﴾ (سورة يوسف: ١٠١)

٢) ﴿ وَرَأَيْتَهُمْ يَصُدُّوْنَ وَهُمْ مُسْتَكْبِرُوْنَ ﴾ (سورة المنافقون: ٥)

٣) ﴿ وَمَا رَبُّكَ بِغَافِلٍ عَمَّا تَعْمَلُوْنَ ﴾ (سورة هود: ١٢٣)

٤) ﴿ فَخَرَجَ مِنْهَا خَائِفًا يَتَرَقَّبُ ﴾ (سورة القصص: ٢١)

٥) ﴿ يَا اَيُّهَا الَّذِيْنَ اٰمَنُوْا إِذَا جَاءَكُمُ الْمُوْمِنَاتِ مُهَاجِرَاتٍ فَامْتَحِنُوْهُنَّ ﴾ (سورة الممتحنة: ١٠)

٦) ﴿ قَالُوْا يَآبَانَا اسْتَغْفِرْ لَنَا ذُنُوْبَنَا اِنَّا كُنَّا خَاطِئِيْنَ ﴾ (سورة يوسف: ٩٧)

٧) ﴿ وَاُولٰئِكَ هُمُ الْمُفْلِحُوْنَ ﴾ (سورة البقرة ٥)

٨) ﴿ كَذٰلِكَ نَجْزِي الْقَوْمَ الْمُجْرِمِيْنَ ﴾ (سورة يونس: ١٣)

٩) ﴿ قَالُوْا اِنَّمَا نَحْنُ مُصْلِحُوْنَ ﴾ (سورة البقرة: ١١)

LESSON 16
THE PASSIVE PARTICIPLE

اِسْمُ الْمَفْعُوْل

A : Vocabulary:

غَلَبَ	نَظَرَ
He overpowered.	He looked.

B : Definition:

اِسْمُ الْمَفْعُوْل : is that noun which explains the person on whom the acton is done. It is an اِسْمُ الْمُشْتَق i.e. a noun derived from a مَصْدَرْ ,

e.g. قَتَلَ زَيْدٌ اَسَدً Zaid killed the lion.

قَاتِلٌ is the killer i.e. Zaid,

مَقْتُوْلٌ is the killed i.e. the lion.

C: The اِسْمُ الْمَفْعُوْل conjugation of triliteral (three lettered) words will be on the scale of: مَفْعُوْلٌ

	MALE	MEANING	FEMALE	MEANING
SINGULAR	مَفْعُوْلٌ	1 male the done upon	مَفْعُوْلَةٌ	1 female done upon
DUAL	مَفْعُوْلَانِ	2 males done upon	مَفْعُوْلَتَانِ	2 females done upon
PLURAL	مَفْعُوْلُوْنَ	Many males done upon	مَفْعُوْلَاتٌ	Many females done upon

The passive participle also does not contain any persons. If so desired, a dhameer (pronoun) can be added before the اِسْمُ الْمَفْعُوْل to denote first, second and third persons.

اَنَا مَنْصُوْرٌ	اَنْتَ مَضْرُوْبٌ	هِيَ مَقْتُوْلَةٌ	هُوَ مَقْتُوْلٌ
نَحْنُ مَنْصُوْرُوْنَ	اَنْتُمَا مَضْرُوْبَانِ	هُمَا مَقْتُوْلَتَانِ	هُمَا مَقْتُوْلَانِ
	اَنْتُمْ مَضْرُوْبُوْنَ	هُنَّ مَقْتُوْلَاتٌ	هُمْ مَقْتُوْلُوْنَ

3.) اِسْمُ الْمَفْعُوْل of an intransitive verb or مَاضِيْ مَضْمُوْمُ الْعَيْن (those past tense verbs that have a dhamma on the عَيْنْ كَلِمَة) does not exist, i.e. there are no such words as مَقْرُوْبٌ مَكْرُوْمٌ

4.) The method of making اِسْمُ الْمَفْعُوْل of a four lettered word or a word that does not have three original letters is similar to that of اِسْمُ الْفَاعِلْ The only difference is that in the اِسْمُ الْفَاعِلْ the عَيْنْ كَلِمَه receives a kasra whereas in the اِسْمُ الْمَفْعُوْل it has fatha,

E.g. مُقْتَنِصٌ (اِسْمُ الْفَاعِلْ) One male hunter

مُقْتَنَصٌ (اِسْمُ الْمَفْعُوْل) One male the hunted.

D: Exercises:

1.) Draw up the اِسْمُ الْمَفْعُوْل conjugation tables of the following :

a.) يَقْتَنِصُ To hunt b.) يُصَرِّفُ To turn c.) يُعَلِّمُ To teach

d.) مَنَعَ e.) آكَلَ f.) غَلَبَ g.) آمَرَ

2.) Change the following into their correct اِسْمُ الْمَفْعُوْل forms. Mention only the singular masculine scale:

a.) All the words listed in your vocabulary thus far.

b.) يُعْلِنُ c.) يُحَرِّمُ d.) يَتَبَاعَدُ e.) يُخَادِعُ f.) يُقَاتِلُ g.) يُقَنْطِرُ

3.) a) Translate the following:

b) Identify the اِسْمُ الْفَاعِلْ or اِسْمُ الْمَفْعُوْل words found in them, mention the mood and topic as well:

١) وَحَالَ بَيْنَهُمَ الْمَوْجُ فَكَانَ مِنَ الْمُغْرَقِيْنَ

٢) كَأَنَّهُمْ بُنْيَانٌ مَرْصُوْصٌ – اِنَّهٗ كَانَ مُخْلَصًا وَكَانَ رَسُوْلًا نَبِيًّا

٣) اِنَّ السَّمْعَ وَالْبَصَرَ وَالْفُؤَادَ كُلُّ اُولٰئِكَ كَانَ مَسْؤُلًا

٤) ضَعُفَ الطَّالِبُ وَالْمَطْلُوْبُ

٥) يَعْلَمُوْنَ اَنَّهٗ مُنَزَّلٌ مِنْ رَبِّكَ بِالْحَقِّ

٦) وَهٰذَا كِتَابٌ اَنْزَلْنَاهُ مُبَارَكٌ مُصَدِّقٌ

4.) Translate:

a.) Two men who were killed.

b.) Many females who are rolled.

c.) One female who is hit.

d.) Two females who are worshipped.

e.) Many doors that are opened.

f.) One (cup of tea) that is drunk.

g.) مُكَذَّبٌ h.) مُسْتَغْفِرُوْنَ i.) مَذْكُوْرَةٌ j.) مَاْخُوْذَتَانِ

k.) مُقْتَنَصٌ l.) مَظْلُوْمَةٌ m.) مَغْسُوْلَانِ n.) مَغْسُوْلَاتٌ

LESSON 17
THE ASYNDETIC RELATIVE CLAUSE

اَلصِّفَةُ الْمُشَبَّهَة

A : Definition:

اَلصِّفَةُ الْمُشَبَّهَة is that noun which indicates a permanent quality. It is made from an intransitive verb,

E.g. جَمِيْلٌ That person who is permanently beautiful.

a.) اَلصِّفَةُ الْمُشَبَّهَة is similar to the active participle (اِسْمُ الْفَاعِل). The only difference is that اِسْمُ الْفَاعِل describes a quality which is temporary and اَلصِّفَةُ الْمُشَبَّهَة describes a quality which is permanent. Thus a person will be called ضَارِبٌ only at the time of hitting. However, a person will be called جَمِيْلٌ at all times. A further example اَلْجُنْدِيُّ شُجَاعٌ The soldier is brave (at all times - a permanent quality).

اَلْجُنْدِيُّ مُقَاتِلٌ The soldier is a fighter (in times of war - a temporary quality).

b.) اَلصِّفَةُ الْمُشَبَّهَة Has many scales, however no fixed rules exist for making the scales. It is sometimes made by adding an الف , واو or ياء after the second original letter. The more common scales are:

1.)	فَعِيْلٌ	شَرِيْفٌ	Noble	سَعِيْدٌ	Fortunate
2.)	فَعُولٌ	وَقُوْرٌ	Dignified	كَسُوْلٌ	Lazy
3.)	فُعَالٌ	شُجَاعٌ	Brave		

Sometimes the original letters remain the same, only the harakaat change:

4.)	فَعَلٌ	حَسَنٌ	Beautiful / good
5.)	فَعِلٌ	فَرِحٌ	Happy
6.)	فَعْلٌ	صَعْبٌ	Hard / difficult
7.)	فُعُلٌ	جُنُبٌ	Impure

c.) A pronoun can be prefixed to the اَلصِّفَةُ الْمُشَبَّهَة to indicate first, second and third person.

هُوَ شَرِيْفٌ   اَنْتَ وَقُوْرٌ   اَنَا شُجَاعٌ

d.) Those verbs that have the meaning of colour, defect and forms of the body will appear on the scale of اَفْعَلُ for masculine words and on the scale of فَعْلَاءُ for feminine words,

E.g.	اَحْمَرُ	Red (man)	حَمْرَاءُ	Red (woman)
	اَعْوَرُ	One - eyed man	عَوْرَاءُ	One - eyed woman
	اَعْيَنُ	Large - eyed man	عَيْنَاءُ	Large - eyed woman

e.) اَلصِّفَةُ الْمُشَبَّهَة has six seghas just like اِسْمُ الْفَاعِل . The signs of dual and plural will be added at the end of the word to create each scale, e.g.

شَرِيْفَةٌ	شَرِيْفٌ
شَرِيْفَتَانِ	شَرِيْفَانِ
شَرِيْفَاتٌ	شَرِيْفُوْنَ

Exercises:

1.) Give the translation, mood and topic of the following:

١) شَجَرَةٌ خَضْرَاءُ

٢) اَلذَّهَبُ اَصْفَرُ وَالْفِضَّةُ بَيْضَاءُ

٣) اَلْعُشْبُ اَخْضَرُ وَالتِّبْنُ اَصْفَرُ

٤) اَلْوَرْدُ اَحْمَرُ اللَّوْنِ وَالطَّيِّبُ الرَّائِحَةِ

٥) اَلْبَحْرُ الْاَحْمَرُ فِيْ غَرْبِ الْعَرَبِ

٦) هٰذِهِ بِنْتٌ سَعِيْدَةٌ وَذٰلِكَ الْوَلَدُ كَسُوْلٌ

٧) اَلْعَبْدُ تَعْبَانٌ وَسَيِّدُهُ غَضْبَانٌ

٨) جَمِيْلٌ اَزْرَقُ الْعَيْنِ وَاَسْوَدُ الشَّعْرِ وَاَبْيَضُ الْوَجْهِ

٩) عَائِشَةُ زَرْقَاءُ الْعَيْنِ وَسَوْدَاءُ الشَّعْرِ وَبَيْضَاءُ الْوَجْهِ

١٠) رَأَيْتُ بِنْتًا حَسَنَةَ الصُّوْرَةِ وَنَظِيفَةَ الثِّيَابِ

١١) فَاطِمَةُ جَمِيْلٌ وَجْهُهَا وَنَظِيْفَةٌ ثِيَابُهَا

١٢) هٰذِهِ الْبَقَرَةُ سَوْدَاءُ عَيْنُهَا وَاَبْيَضُ رَأْسُهَا

١٣) زَيْدٌ حَسَنُ الْوَجْهِ وَقَبِيْحُ الثِّيَابِ

١٤) عَمْرٌو حَسَنٌ وَجْهُهُ وَقَبِيْحَةٌ ثِيَابُهُ

١٥) تِلْكَ النِّسَاءُ خُرْصٌ وَهٰذِهِ عَمْيَاءُ

١٦) فِي الْبُسْتَانِ اَزْهَارٌ حُمْرٌ وَصُفْرٌ وَطُيُوْرٌ بِيْضٌ وَسُوْدٌ

١٧) وَجْنَتَا الْبِنْتِ الْحَمْرَاوَانِ لَطِيْفَتَا الْمَنْظَرِ

١٨) اِنَّ زُبَيْدَةَ وَرَشِيْدًا كِلَيْهِمَا صَالِحَانِ وَحَسَنَ الْخُلْقِ

١٩) صَدِيْقِيْ خَلِيْلٌ رَجُلٌ سَهِلٌ طَلِقٌ

٢٥) اَلْكُفَّارُ هُمْ صُمٌّ بُكْمٌ عُمْيٌ فَهُمْ لَا يَعْقِلُوْنَ

٢١) اِنَّهُ كَانَ ظَلُوْمًا جَهُوْلًا

٢٢) حُوْرٌ عِيْنٌ كَاَمْثَالِ اللُّؤْلُؤِ الْمَكْنُوْنِ

2.) Fill in the blanks:

١) لَوْنُ اللَّبَنِ ______ وَلَوْنُ ______ اَحْمَرُ

٢) اَللَّبَنُ ______ وَالْعَسَلُ ______

٣) اَللَّبَنُ ______ اللَّوْنِ وَالْعَسَلُ ______ اللَّوْنِ

٤) اَوْرَاقُ الرُّمَّانِ ______ وَاَزْهَارُهُ ______

٥) اَمَامَ بَيْتِيْ شَجَرَةٌ ______

٦) هِرَّةُ اُخْتِيْ ______

٧) رَأَيْتُ هِرَّتَيْنِ ______

٨) هٰذَا وَلَدٌ ______ الْوَجْهِ وَ ______ الْعَيْنِ

٩) هٰذَا الْوَلَدُ حَسَنٌ ______ وَقَبِيْحَةٌ ______

١٠) رَأَيْتُ بِنْتًا اَبْيَضَ ______ وَ ______ عَيْنُهَا

١١) لَوْنُ وَجْهُ رُقَيَّةَ ______وَلَوْنُ شَعْرِهَا ______

١٢) هِيَ بَيْضَاءُ ______وَسَوْدَاء ______

١٣) هٰذَا الْوَلَدُ زَرْقَاوَانِ ______

١٤) عِنْدِيْ ______بَيْضَاءُوَبَقَرَةٌ ______

LESSON 18
THE SUPERLATIVE NOUN (EXAGGERATION, HYPERBOLE)

اِسْمُ الْمُبَالَغَةْ

Definition:

اِسْمُ الْمُبَالَغَةْ is that اِسْمُ الْمُشْتَق (derivative) which emphasizes an action in itself. It shows intensity in meaning,

E.g. ضَرَّابْ One who hits excessively.

a.) There are no fixed laws for making اِسْمُ الْمُبَالَغَةْ as most of the scales are سِمَاعِئ (heard from the Arabs.) Nevertheless, it is generally made by adding an الف , واو or ياء after the second original letter, or by repeating one of the original letters. The most commonly used scales are:

1.)	فَعِيْلٌ	عَلِيْمٌ	One who is extremely knowledgeable.
2.)	فُعُوْلٌ	اَكُوْلٌ	One who eats alot (glutton).
3.)	فَعُّوْلٌ	قَيُّوْمٌ	One who establishes very well / one who maintains very well.
4.)	فُعَّلٌ	قُلَّبٌ	Very versatile.
5.)	فَعِلٌ	حَذِرٌ	Very watchful.

b.) اِسْمُ الْمُبَالَغَةْ has a singular, dual and plural for each scale,

E.g. فَعَّالٌ فَعَّالَانِ فَعَّالُوْنَ

c.) The scales for اِسْمُ الْمُبَالَغَةْ are common for both masculine and feminine.

E.g. هِيَ عَلِيْمٌ - هُوَ عَلِيْمٌ

d.) Sometimes a ة is added at the end of اِسْمُ الْمُبَالَغَةْ but does not denote femininity. The additional ة is merely for emphasis and exaggeration.

E.g. هُوَ عَلَّامَةٌ - هِيَ عَلَّامَةٌ

e.) When the meaning of trade or profession is intended, the scale فَعَّالٌ will be used but it will not denote an exaggerated meaning.

E.g. خَيَّاطٌ Tailor; بَزَّارٌ Seedsman; جَمَّالٌ Camel driver

بَقَّالٌ Grocer; حَجَّامٌ Cupper of blood

Exercise:

1.) Translate the following and state what type of ism each one is:

a.) مِنْطِيْقٌ	b.) صِدِّيْقٌ	c.) ضُحْكَةٌ	d.) اَعْرَجُ	e.) قُلَّبَانِ
f.) اَسْوَدُ	g.) قُدُّوْسٌ	h.) حَدَّادٌ	i.) مِجْزَمٌ	j.) اَبْكَمُ
k.) قَتِيْلٌ	l.) اَطْرَشُ	m.) نَجَّارَانِ	n.) اَزْرَقُ	o.) لَطِيْفٌ
p.) اَحْدَبُ	q.) بَنَّاؤُوْنَ	r.) جَلَّادٌ	s.) سَفَّاكٌ	

LESSON 19
THE COMPARATIVE NOUN (ELATIVE)

اِسْمُ التَّفْضِيلْ

A : Vocabulary:

قَلَّ	قَرُبَ	نَظُفَ
It was less.	He was near.	He was clean.

B : Definition:

اِسْمُ التَّفْضِيلْ : is that noun which compares two things. It gives the meaning of better than / greater than.

E.g. اَللّٰهُ اَكْبَرُ Allah is not merely great but He is greater than everything else.

The difference between اِسْمُ التَّفْضِيلْ (Elative) and اِسْمُ الْمُبَالَغَةْ (Superlative) is that اِسْمُ الْمُبَالَغَةْ emphasizes something in itself however, اِسْمُ التَّفْضِيلْ compares the greatness between two things.

E.g زَيْدٌ ضَرَّابٌ - Zaid hits a lot. زَيْدٌ اَضْرَبُ مِنْ عَمْرٍو - Zaid hits more than Amr.

The scales of اِسْمُ التَّفْضِيلْ are:

One male who does more than	وَاحِدْ مُذَكَّرْ	اَفْعَلُ
Two males who do more than	تَثْنِيَه مُذَكَّرْ	اَفْعَلَانِ
Many males who do more than	جَمَعْ مُذَكَّرْ	اَفْعَلُوْنَ / اَفَاعِلُ
One female who does more than	وَاحِدْ مُؤَنَّثْ	فُعْلَى
Two females who do more than	تَثْنِيَه مُؤَنَّثْ	فُعْلَيَانِ
Many females who do more than	جَمَعْ مُؤَنَّثْ	فُعْلَيَاتٌ / فُعَلٌ

1.) مِنْ is usually used as a صِلَة for اِسْمُ التَّفْضِيلْ , i.e. it usually follows اِسْمُ التَّفْضِيلْ
E.g. زَيْدٌ اَحْسَنُ مِنْ عَمْرٍو - Zaid is better than Amr.

2.) اِسْمُ التَّفْضِيلْ never gets a tanween at the end. (This excludes the feminine plural form).

3.) اِسْمُ التَّفْضِيلْ generally gives the meaning of the فَاعِلٌ (doer).
E.g. اَنْصَرُ One who helps more than .(نَاصِرٌ)
However, it sometimes gives the meaning of the مَفْعُوْلٌ (object).
E.g. اَشْهَرُ - more famous (مَشْهُوْرٌ) اَشْغَلُ - more engrossed. (مَشْغُوْلٌ)

4.) اِسْمُ التَّفْضِيلْ does not give the meaning of colour or defect. Therefore although اَسْوَدُ (black) (not more black) and اَعْوَرُ (one - eyed) are on the scale of اَفْعَلُ yet they are not regarded as اِسْمُ التَّفْضِيلْ . They fall under اَلصِّفَةُ الْمُشَبَّهَة .

5.) The above scales of اِسْمُ التَّفْضِيْل are for ثُلَاثِيْ مُجَرَّد (triliteral words i.e. three lettered original words) only. If اِسْمُ التَّفْضِيْل of a four lettered word is desired then words such as اَكْثَرُ , اَشَدُّ or اَكْبَرُ should be added before the مَصْدَر of the intended word.

E.g. زَيْدٌ اَكْثَرُ اِجْتِهَادًا مِنْ عَمْرٍووَاَقَلُّ اِكْتِسَابٍ مِنْ بَكْرٍ

Zaid is more hardworking than Amr and earns less than Bakr.

6.) The words خَيْرٌ and شَرٌّ are also regarded as اِسْمُ التَّفْضِيْل .

E.g.	اَنَا خَيْرٌ مِنْهُ	-	I am better than him.
	هُمْ شَرُّ الْخَلْقِ	-	They are the worst of the creation.

Exercises:

1.) Draw up the conjugation tables of the comparative noun for the following words:

a.) بَعُدَ b.) قَرُبَ c.) حَسُنَ d.) سَأَلَ

2.) Translate:

a.) اَنْعَمَانِ	b.) اَمَانِعُ	c.) نُصْرٰى	d.) شُكْرٰى	e.) اَذْكَرَانِ
f.) ظُلَّمٌ	g.) اُمْرٰى	h.) ضُحْكَيَانِ	i.) قُرْآيَاتٌ	j.) اَسْرَعُ
k.) اَقَالِبُ	l.) ضُرْبٰى	m.) اَلْاَعْلٰى	n.) اَحْمَرُ	o.) اَحَقُّ
p.) اَعْرَجُ	q.) اَتْقٰى	r.) اَضَاحِكُ	s.) اَوْهَنُ	

3.) Identify all the comparative nouns. Write the singular, masculine and feminine forms with translation:

١) ﴿ وَمِنْكُمْ مَنْ يُرَدُّ اِلٰى اَرْذَلِ الْعُمُرِ ﴾(سورة النحل: ٧٠)

٢) ﴿ اِنَّ رَبَّكَ هُوَ اَعْلَمُ بِمَنْ ضَلَّ عَنْ سَبِيْلِهٖ وَهُوَ اَعْلَمُ بِالْمُهْتَدِيْنَ ﴾ (سورة النحل: ١٢٠)

٣) ﴿ وَلَعَذَابُ الْاٰخِرَةِ اَكْبَرُ ﴾ (سورة القلم: ٣٣)

٤) ﴿ قُلْ نَارُ جَهَنَّمَ اَشَدُّ حَرًّا ﴾ (سورة التوبة: ٨١)

٥) ﴿ مِنْ اٰيَاتِنَا الْكُبْرٰى ﴾ (سورة طٰه: ٢٣)

٦) ﴿ وَصَدَّقَ بِالْحُسْنٰى ﴾ (سورة اليل: ٦)

4.) Translate into Arabic:

a.) One male who desires more

b.) Two females who eat more than

c.) Two females who are more hounoured

d.) Many males who are more virtuous

e.) Many females who are more tall

f.) One male who is more short

g.) Many males who recite more than

h.) Two females who command more

i.) One female who separates more

j.) One female who refrains more.

5.) Give the translation, mood and topic for the following:

١) سُبْحَانَ رَبِّيَ الْاَعْلٰى

٢) اَلصَّلَاةُ خَيْرٌ مِنَ النَّوْمِ

٣) اَقْبَحُ النَّاسِ الرَّجُلُ الْجَهُوْلُ الْكَسُوْلُ

٤) اَفْضَلُ الْاَعْمَالِ الصَّلَاةُ لِوَقْتِهَا

٥) اَفْضَلُ الْمُوْمِنِيْنَ اَحْسَنُهُمْ خُلُقًا

٦) خَيْرُ النَّاسِ مَنْ يَّنْفَعُ النَّاسَ

٧) اَلْمَدْرَسَةُ الْكُبْرٰى فِى الْجَامِعِ الْاَزْهَرِ

٨) شَوْقِىْ اِلَيْكَ اَشَدُّ مِنْهُ اِلٰى اَخِيْكَ

٩) اَلرِّيْحُ الْيَوْمَ اَشَدُّ مِنْهَا الْبَارِحَةَ

١٠) حَاتِمٌ قَلِيْلُ الْعَقْلِ وَاَخُوْهُ اَقَلُّ الْعَقْلِ مِنْهُ

١١) اَلْحِكْمَةُ ضَالَّةُ الْمُوْمِنِ فَحَيْثُ وَجَدَهَا فَهُوَ اَحَقُّ بِهَا

١٢) خِيَارُكُمْ فِى الْجَاهِلِيَّةِ خِيَارُكُمْ فِى الْاِسْلَامِ

١٤) اَلْحَسَنُ صَدِيْقُ حَسَنٍ وَمُحَمَّدٌ اَحْسَنُ مِنْهُ هُوَ اَحْسَنُ اَصْدِقَائِىْ

And from the Qur'aan:

١) ﴿اِنَّ اَكْرَمَكُمْ عِنْدَ اللهِ اَتْقٰكُمْ﴾ (سورة الحجرات: ١٣)

٢) ﴿وَالْفِتْنَةُ اَكْبَرُ مِنَ الْقَتْلِ﴾ (سورة البقرة: ١٩١)

٣) ﴿قُلْ ءَاَنْتُمْ اَعْلَمُ اَمِ اللهُ﴾ (سورة البقرة: ١٤٠)

٤) ﴿وَلَعَبْدٌ مُّوْمِنٌ خَيْرٌ مِّنْ مُّشْرِكٍ﴾ (سورة البقرة: ٢٢١)

٥) ﴿وَلَاَمَةٌ مُّوْمِنَةٌ خَيْرٌ مِّنْ مُّشْرِكَةٍ﴾ (سورة البقرة: ٢٢١)

٦) ﴿فَاَىُّ الْفَرِيْقَيْنِ اَحَقُّ بِالْاَمْنِ﴾ (سورة الانعام:٨١)

٧) ﴿اَلَا لَهُ الْحُكْمُ وَهُوَ اَسْرَعُ الْحَاسِبِيْنَ﴾ (سورة الانعام:٦٢)

٨) ﴿يَسْأَلُوْنَكَ عَنِ الْخَمْرِ وَالْمَيْسِرِ قُلْ فِيْهِمَا اِثْمٌ كَبِيْرٌ وَمَنَافِعُ لِلنَّاسِ وَاِثْمُهُمَا اَكْبَرُ مِنْ نَّفْعِهِمَا﴾ (سورة البقرة: ٢١٩)

٩) ﴿ اِنَّ اَوْهَنَ الْبُيُوْتِ لَبَيْتُ الْعَنْكَبُوْتِ ﴾ (سورة العنكبوت: ٤١)

١٠) ﴿هُمْ لِلْكُفْرِ يَوْمَئِذٍ اَقْرَبُ مِنْهُمْ لِلْاِيْمَانِ ﴾ (سورة الانعام: ١٦٧)

١١) ﴿ اَلَيْسَ اللهُ بِاَحْكَمِ الْحَاكِمِيْنَ ﴾ (سورة التين: ٨) بَلٰى هُوَ اَحْكَمُ الْحَاكِمِيْنَ - وَنَحْنُ عَلٰى ذٰلِكَ مِنَ الشَّاهِدِيْنَ

LESSON 20
ADVERB DENOTING TIME OR PLACE
اِسْمُ الظَّرْف

A : Vocabulary:

قَعَدَ / جَلَسَ	سَأَلَ	طَبَخَ
He sat.	He asked.	He cooked.

B: Definition:

اِسْمُ الظَّرْف is that noun which gives us an idea of the time or place in which an action occurs.

اِسْمُ الظَّرْف is of two types:

i.) ظَرْفُ الْمَكَان - refers to the place of where an action occurs.

ii.) ظَرْفُ الزَّمَان - refers to the time when an action occurs.

e.g. مَلْعَبٌ - One place of playing

مَطْبَخٌ - One place of cooking.

مَقْعَدٌ - One place or time of sitting.

1.) اِسْمُ الظَّرْف is made by adding a مِيْمُ الْمَفْتُوْح (مَ) to the مَصْدَرْ (root word).

e.g. مَضْرِبٌ - time or place of hitting.

2.) اِسْمُ الظَّرْف appears in either of the following two scales:

1) مَفْعِلٌ 2) مَفْعَلٌ

3.) The conjugation is as follows:

TRANSLATION	SCALE 1	SCALE 2
1 time / place of doing	مَفْعَلٌ	مَفْعِلٌ
2 times / places of doing	مَفْعَلَانِ	مَفْعِلَانِ
Many times / places of doing	مَفَاعِلُ	مَفَاعِلُ

The جَمع is common for both مُذَكَّر and مُؤَنَّث .

4.) If مُضَارِع is مَفْتُوحُ الْعَيْن or مَضْمُوْمُ الْعَيْن then the word will have a fatha on the (middle radical).

If مُضَارِع is مَكْسُوْرُ الْعَيْنْ then the عِيْن كَلْمَه of اِسْمُ الظَّرْف will have a kasra.

E.g يَنْصُرُ will become مَنْصَرٌ

يَضْرِبُ will become مَضْرِبٌ

يَفْتَحُ will become مَفْتَحٌ

5.) There are twelve words in the Arabic language which are مُضَارِعْ مَضْمُوْمُ الْعَيْن but have a kasra on the عَيْن كَلِمَه. The twelve exceptions are:

1.)	مَنْسِكٌ	Place of slaughter.
2.)	مَجْزِرٌ	Slaughterhouse.
3.)	مَنْبِتٌ	Place of growing (farm).
4.)	مَطْلِعٌ	Place of rising.
5.)	مَشْرِقٌ	Place where sun rises (east).
6.)	مَغْرِبٌ	Place where sun sets (west).
7.)	مَفْرِقٌ	Place of separating i.e. the line separating the hair of the head.
8.)	مَسْقِطٌ	Place of falling.
9.)	مَسْكِنٌ	Place of living.
10.)	مَرْفِقٌ	Place of comfort (i.e. anything from which benefit is derived).
11.)	مَسْجِدٌ	Place of prostrating.
12.)	مَنْخِرٌ	Nostril.

The above scales are for triliteral verbs only. If اِسْمُ الظَّرْفْ of a four lettered word is desired then it will be on the scale of اِسْمُ الْمَفْعُوْل i.e. مُفْعَلْ

E.g. مُكْرَمٌ Place of honour / hospitality,
مُخْرَجٌ Place of removal / extraction.

Exercises:

1.) Place the following words on the scale of اِسْمُ الظَّرْفْ :

a.) طَبَخَ b.) قَعَدَ c.) جَلَسَ d.) غَسَلَ

2.) Translate the following into Arabic:

A.) Two places of eating.

b.) One place of washing.

c.) Many places of drinking.

d.) One place of hitting.

f.) Many places of oppressing.

g.) Many places of opening.

h.) Many places of mocking.

3.) Translate the following:

a.) مَلَاعِبُ b.) مَطْعَمَانِ c.) مَدَارِسُ d.) مَنْظَرٌ e.) مَدَاخِلُ

f.) مَفْصِلَانِ g.) مَجَالِسُ h.) مَنْزِلٌ i.) مَخْزَنٌ j.) مَوْقِفٌ

k.) مَرْقَنٌ l.) مَكَاتِبُ m.) مَظَالِمُ n.) مَرْقَدٌ o.) مَزْرَعَةٌ

p.) مَصْنَعٌ q.) مَعْمَلٌ r.) مَنْفَعٌ

4.) Identify the nouns and verbs in the following ayaat.
State the mood and topic of each word:

١) ﴿ حَتَّىٰ زُرْتُمُ الْمَقَابِرَ ﴾ (سورة التكاثر: ٢)

٢) ﴿ وَسَكَنتُمْ فِي مَسَاكِنِ الَّذِينَ ﴾ (سورة إبراهيم: ٤٥)

٣) ﴿ وَلَهُمْ فِيهَا مَنَافِعُ وَمَشَارِبُ ﴾ (سورة يس: ٧٣)

LESSON 21
TOOL OR INSTRUMENT

اِسْمُ الْآلَة

A : Vocabulary:

مَلَكَ	بَلَغَ	دَرَسَ
He owned.	He reached.	He learnt.

B: Definition:

اِسْمُ الْآلَة is that noun which names the tool or instrument with which some work is done.

E.g. مَضْرِبٌ Instrument of hitting.

1.) اِسْمُ الْآلَة has three scales in which there is no difference between the masculine and feminine i.e. it is common for both.

2.) The gardaan is as follows:

PLURAL	DUAL	SINGULAR	
مَفَاعِلُ	مِفْعَلَانِ	مِفْعَلٌ	1
مَفَاعِلُ	مِفْعَلَتَانِ	مِفْعَلَةٌ	2
مَفَاعِيْلُ	مِفْعَالَانِ	مِفْعَالٌ	3

3.) a.) The first scale of اِسْمُ الْآلَة is made by adding a اَلْمِيْمُ الْمَكْسُوْر (مِ) before the مَصْدَر

E.g. مِضْرَبٌ

b.) The second scale is made by adding a ة at the end of the first scale.

E.g. مِضْرَبَةٌ

c.) The third scale is made by adding an alif after the عَيْن كَلْمَه

E.g. مِضْرَابٌ

4.) Example of the first scale: مِخْيَطٌ Instrument of sewing i.e. needle.

Example of the second scale: مِرْوَحَةٌ Instrument of giving wind i.e. a fan

Example of the third scale: مِفْتَاحٌ Instrument of opening i.e. a key

مِقْرَاظٌ Instrument of cutting i.e. a pair of scissors

5.) Alternatively:

a.) Change the word to مُضَارِعْ — E.g يَنْصُرُ

b.) Remove the yaa — نْصُرُ

c.) Replace it with a اَلْمِيْمُ الْمَكْسُوْر — مِنْصُرُ

d.) Give the عَيْن كَلْمَه مِنْصَرٌ a fatha — مِنْصَرُ

e.) Give the last letter a tanween — مِنْصَرٌ

6.) The above laws are for three lettered words only. If إِسْمُ الْآلَة of a four lettered word is desired then the words مَابِه will be added before the مَصْدَرْ .

E.g. مَابِه الْاِنْفِطَارُ — Instrument of cracking / breaking apart.

مَابِهِ الْاِقْتِنَاصُ — Instrument of hunting.

Exercises:

1.) Draw up the conjugation table for the following:

a.) ضَرَبَ b.) دَخَلَ c.) قَعَدَ d.) طَبَخَ e.) صَرَفَ

3.) Translate the following:

a.) مَزَامِيْرُ b.) مَغْسِلٌ c.) مِقْتَلَانِ d.) مِغْسَلٌ e.) مِأْكَلٌ

f.) مِكْنَسَةٌ g.) مَآرِبُ h.) مِسْطَرٌ i.) مِنْصَرَةٌ j.) مِكْيَالٌ

k.) مِشْرَبَتَانِ l.) مِنْشَارٌ m.) مَغْسَلَانِ n.) مِطْرَقَةٌ

3.) Give the Arabic of the following:

a.) One instrument of oppressing.

b.) Many instruments of killing.

c.) Two instruments of wearing.

d.) Many instruments of playing.

e.) Two instruments of reciting.

4.) Identify the derivative nouns and mention the mood and topic:

١) اَنَا ذَاهِبٌ غَدًا اِلَى حَيْدَرْآبَادْ

٢) هُمَا ذَاهِبَانِ اِلَى دِهْلِي

٣) هُمْ ذَاهِبُوْنَ اِلَى مَدْرَاس

٤) هٰؤُلَاءِ الْبَنَاتُ ذَاهِبَاتٌ اِلَى لَاهُوْرَ

٥) اَخِيْ كَانَ ذَاهِبًا اِلَى بُمْبَائِيْ اَمْسِ

٦) نَحْنُ كُنَّا نَاجِحِيْنَ

٧) هٰذِهِ مَدْرَسَةٌ وَتِلْكَ مَكْتَبَةٌ وَذٰلِكَ مَسْجِدٌ

٨) اَلْمَدْرَسَةُ مَفْتُوْحَةٌ

٩) هَلْ عِنْدَكَ مِفْتَاحُ هٰذَا الْبَيْتِ ؟

١٠) نَعَمْ عِنْدِيْ مِفْتَاحُهُ

١١) إِذًا لِمَ لَاتَفْتَحُ الْبَابَ ؟

١٢) اَلْبَابُ مَفْتُوْحٌ لٰكِنَّ الدُّخُوْلَ فِيْ هٰذَا الْبَيْتِ مَمْنُوْعٌ

١) فَاتِحُ مِصْرَ هُوَ عَمْرُو بْنُ الْعَاصِ الَّذِىْ فَتَحَهَا فِىْ سَنَةِ عِشْرِيْنَ مِنَ الْهِجْرَةِ

٢) اَلْحَدَّادُ يَطْرُقُ الْحَدِيْدَ بِالْمِطْرَقَةِ وَيَصْنَعُ مِنْهُ الْمَفَاتِيْحَ وَالْاَقْفَالَ وَالْمَنَاجِلَ وَالسَّكَاكِيْنَ

٣) اَلنَّجَّارُ يَقْطَعُ الْخَشَبَ بِالْمِنْشَارِ لِيَصْنَعَ مِنْهُ الْكَرَاسِىَّ وَالطَّوَالَاتِ وَالْمَقَاعِدَ

٤) سَمِعْنَا اَنَّ حُكُوْمَةَ الْجَلَالَةِ الْمَلِكِ النِّظَامِ عُثْمَانَ عَلِى خَانَ قَدْفَتَحَ مَعَامِلَ وَمَصَانِعَ عَدِيْدَةً تُنْسَجُ فِىْ بَعْضِهَا الثِّيَابُ وَتُصْنَعُ فِىْ بَعْضِهَا اٰلَاتُ الْحَرْبِ

٥) يَاحَبِيْبِىْ يَلْزَمُ عَلَيْكَ الْاِعْتِدَالُ فِى الْمَأْكَلِ وَالْمَشْرَبِ كَىْ لَاتَكُوْنَ مَرِيْضًا

٦) كَانَ ذٰلِكَ الرَّجُلُ شَارِبَ الْخَمْرِ فَلَمَّا قَرَأَ الْقُرْاٰنَ وَفَهِمَ مَوَاعِظَهُ صَلُحَ حَالُهُ

٧) اَلدُّنْيَا مَزْرَعَةُ الْاٰخِرَةِ

From the Qur'aan:

١) ﴿ اَلْحَمْدُ لِلّٰهِ الَّذِي خَلَقَ السَّمٰوَاتِ وَالْاَرْضَ وَجَعَلَ الظُّلُمَاتِ وَالنُّوْرَ ﴾ (سورة الانعام: ١)

٢) ﴿ قَالَ اِنِّىْ جَاعِلُكَ لِلنَّاسِ اِمَامًا ﴾ (سورة البقرة: ١٢٤)

٣) ﴿ وَالسَّارِقُ وَالسَّارِقَةُ فَاقْطَعُوْا اَيْدِيَهُمَا ﴾ (سورة المائدة: ٣٨)

٤) ﴿ فِيْهَا عَيْنٌ جَارِيَةٌ فِيْهَا سُرُرٌ مَرْفُوْعَةٌ وَّاَكْوَابٌ مَّوْضُوْعَةٌ ﴾ (سورة الغاشية: ١٢- ١٤)

٥) ﴿ وَلَاتَنْقُصُ الْمِكْيَالَ وَالْمِيْزَانَ ﴾ (سورة هود: ٨٤)

٦) ﴿ وَلَهُمْ فِيْهَا مَنَافِعُ وَمَشَارِبُ اَفَلَا يَشْكُرُوْنَ ﴾ (سورة يٰس: ٧٣)

٧) ﴿ اِنَّ مَوْعِدَهُمُ الصُّبْحُ اَلَيْسَ الصُّبْحُ بِقَرِيْبٍ ﴾ (سورة هود: ٨١)

A COMPREHENSIVE DIAGRAM OF THE SCALES OF DERIVATIVE NOUNS:

اَلْأَسْمَاءُ الْمُشْتَقَّة	3 LETTERED VERBS	4 LETTERED VERBS	TRANSLATION
اِسْمُ الْفَاعِل	فَاعِلٌ	مُفْعِلٌ	1 male doer
اِسْمُ الْمَفْعُوْل	مَفْعُوْلٌ	مُفْعَلٌ	1 male done upon
اِسْمُ الظَّرْف	مَفْعَلٌ / مَفْعِلٌ	مُفْعَلٌ	1 time / place of doing
اِسْمُ الْآلَة	مِفْعَلٌ / مِفْعَلَةٌ / مِفْعَالٌ	مَابِه + مَصْدَرْ	1 instrument of doing
اِسْمُ التَّفْضِيْل	اَفْعَلُ (مُذَكَّرٌ) / فُعْلَى (مُؤَنَّث)	اَشَدُّ / اَكْبَرُ + مَصْدَرْ	1 who does more than

LESSON 22
PRIMARY AND DERIVED FORMS

اَلْمُجَرَّدْ وَالْمَزِيْدْ فِيْه

A : Vocabulary:

تَبَخْتَرَ	دَحْرَجَ	تَرْجَمَ	بَعْثَرَ
He walked with pride.	He rolled.	He translated.	He scattered.

B: Definition:

1.) ثُلَاثِيْ - A triliteral verb i.e. a verb with three letters.

e.g. فَهِمَ - He understood سَجَنَ - He imprisoned

2.) رُبَاعِيْ - A quadriliteral verb i.e. a verb with four letters.

e.g. زَلْزَلَ - He shook, he caused to tremble بَعْثَرَ - He scattered.

3.) مُجَرَّدْ (The primary / stripped form) - A word which consists of original letters only. It contains no extra letters. e.g. جَرَحَ - He wounded contains three original letters. It is therefore termed ثُلَاثِيْ مُجَرَّدْ (thulaathie mujarrad). Other examples of ثُلَاثِيْ مُجَرَّدْ are:

دَخَلَ He entered ذَهَبَ He went خَسَفَ It sank / He caused to sink.

حَصْحَصَ - (It became evident) contains four original letters. It is therefore termed رُبَاعِيْ مُجَرَّدْ (rubaaie mujarrad). Other examples of rubaaie mujarrad are:

دَحْرَجَ He rolled تَرْجَمَ He translated

4.) مَزِيْدْ فِيْه (The increased form) refers to such a word which contains original letters as well as extra letters e.g. اَسْلَمَ - He submitted it contains three original letters i.e. سَلَمَ And has one extra letter i.e. alif. It is thus categorized as ثُلَاثِيْ مَزِيْدْ فِيْه (Thulaathie mazeed fee). Other examples of ثُلَاثِيْ مَزِيْدْ فِيْه are:

اِسْتَغْفَرَ He sought forgiveness اِنْفَطَرَ It / he broke apart صَرَّفَ He turned

تَبَخْتَرَ - He walked with pride. This word contains four original letters i.e. بَخْتَرَ And has one extra letter i.e. the first ت . It is thus categorized as رُبَاعِيْ مَزِيْدْ فِيْه (rubaaie mazeed feeh).

Other examples of rubaaie mazeed feeh are:

تَسَرْبَلَ He dressed اِحْرَنْجَمَ He gathered (it got together) تَبَرْقَعَ He wore a burqa (veil).

5.) هَمْزَةُ الْوَصْل - a temporary hamza which is written but not read when joined to another word.

e.g. فَاصْبِرْ ، ثُمَّ انْصُرْ

C1: The Arabic language is rich in derived forms which extend or modify the meaning of the root form of the verb giving many shades of meaning.

E.g. 1.) كَتَبَ means to write, كَاتَبَ means to write to or to correspond with, تَكَاتَبَ means to write to each other or to correspond with each other.

2.) قَتَلَ means to kill, قَتَّلَ means to massacre and قَاتَلَ to fight.

3.) كَسَرَ to break, اِنْكَسَرَ and تَكَسَّرَ to be broken.

4.)	i	قَبِلَ	to accept; to draw near
	iv	اَقْبَلَ	to approach or to turn forward
	v	تَقَبَّلَ	to receive or grant
	ii	قَبَّلَ	to kiss
	vi	تَقَابَلَ	to meet or to be compared to or to face
	iii	قَابَلَ	to face or to comfort
	viii	اِقْتَبَلَ	to receive or to apply
	x	اِسْتَقْبَلَ	to receive (a visitor)

C2:

Verbs contain either three original letters or four original letters. Both three and four original lettered verbs are divided into mujarrad (the primary form) and mazeed feeh (the drived form). There are thus four classifications of verbs:

i) ثُلَاثِيْ مُجَرَّدْ	E.g.	فَعَلَ	ذَهَبَ
ii.) ثُلَاثِيْ مَزِيْد فِيْه	E.g.	اَفْعَلَ	اَسْلَمَ
iii.) رُبَاعِيْ مُجَرَّدْ	E.g.	فَعْلَلَ	دَحْرَجَ
iv رُبَاعِيْ مَزِيْد فِيْه	E.g.	تَفَعْلَلَ	تَبَخْتَرَ

Verbs are divided into scales as follows:

a.) ثُلَاثِيْ مُجَرَّدْ i.) Has six scales:

EXAMPLE	SCALE	ABBREVIATION	ARABIC ABBREVIATION
عَبَدَ يَعْبُدُ	نَصَرَ يَنْصُرُ	U	(ن)
مَلَكَ يَمْلِكُ	ضَرَبَ يَضْرِبُ	I	(ض)
لَعِبَ يَلْعَبُ	سَمِعَ يَسْمَعُ	A	(س)
سَاَلَ يَسْاَلُ	فَتَحَ يَفْتَحُ	A	(ف)
صَغُرَ يَصْغُرُ	كَرُمَ يَكْرُمُ	U	(ك)
نَعِمَ يَنْعِمُ	حَسِبَ يَحْسِبُ	I	(ح)

b.) ثُلَاثِيْ مَزِيْد فِيْهِ has fourteen scales:

i.) 9 scales begin with a هَمْزَةُ الْوَصْل ,

	SCALE	EXAMPLE	TRANSLATION	Dictionary no.
1	اِفْتِعَال	اِجْتِنَابٌ	to refrain	viii
2	اِسْتِفْعَال	اِسْتِغْفَارٌ	to repent	x
3	اِنْفِعَال	اِنْفِطَارٌ	to crack	vii
4	اِفْعِلَال	اِحْمِرَارٌ	to be red in colour	ix
5	اِفْعِيْلَال	اِدْهِيْمَامٌ	to be black in colour	xiii
6	اِفْعِيْعَال	اِخْشِيْشَانٌ	to be rough	xiii
7	اِفْعِوَّال	اِجْلِوَّاذٌ	to run; to hasten	
8	اِفَّعُّلٌ was originally on the scale تَفَعُّلٌ *	اِطَّهُّرٌ	to be pure	
9	اِتَّاعُلٌ was originally on the scale تَفَاعُلٌ *	اِثَّاقُلٌ	to be heavy	

* Both these scales will be mentioned in the forthcoming pages.

ii.) Five scales do not have a هَمْزَةُ الْوَصْل ,

	SCALE	EXAMPLE	TRANSLATION	Dictionary no.
1	اِفْعَالٌ	اِكْرَامٌ	to honour	iv
2	تَفْعِيْلٌ	تَصْرِيْفٌ	to turn	ii
3	مُفَاعَلَةٌ	مُقَاتَلَةٌ	to fight	iii
4	تَفَعُّلٌ	تَقَبُّلٌ	to accept	v
5	تَفَاعُلٌ	تَعَارُفٌ	to recognize	vi

c.) رُبَاعِيْ مُجَرَّدْ has one scale only,

	SCALE	EXAMPLE	TRANSLATION
1	فَعْلَلَةٌ	دَحْرَجَةٌ	to roll

d.) رُبَاعِيْ مَزِيْد فِيْهِ has three scales,

i.) Two scales have a هَمْزَةُ الْوَصْل ,

	SCALE	EXAMPLE	TRANSLATION	Dictionary no.
1	اِفْعِنْلَالٌ	اِحْرِنْجَامٌ	to gather; to come together	xiv
2	اِفْعِلَّالٌ	اِزْمِهْرَارٌ	for eyes to be red	

ii.) One scale does not begin with a هَمْزَةُ الْوَصْل ,

	SCALE	EXAMPLE	TRANSLATION	Dictionary no.
1	تَفَعْلُلٌ	تَسَرْبُلٌ	to dress	xiv

Note 1: مَصْدَرْ is that word from which nouns and verbs are derived. It gives the meaning of 'to' or 'ing' when translated into English.

E.g. ضَرَبَ to hit or hitting نَصَرَ to help or helping.

Note 2: The scales of ثُلَاثِيْ مَزِيْد فِيْه , رُبَاعِيْ مُجَرَّدْ and رُبَاعِيْ مَزِيْد فِيْه are named after the (root word) of each scale.

E.g. The word اِنْفَطَرَ will fall under the scale of اِنْفِعَالْ because the مَصْدَرْ is اِنْفِطَارْ. The مَصْدَرْ `s of ثُلَاثِيْ مَزِيْد فِيْه , رُبَاعِيْ مُجَرَّدْ and رُبَاعِيْ مَزِيْد فِيْه are fixed.

Note 3: ثُلَاثِيْ مُجَرَّدْ has more than fifty مَصَادِرْ. Each scale is named after the singular masculine third person (وَاحِدْ مُذَكَّرْ غَائِبْ) of مَاضِيْ e.g. عَبَدَ is from بَابْ نَصَرَ .

LESSON 23
THE CONDENSED CONJUGATION OF THE SIX ثُلَاثِيْ مُجَرَّدْ SCALES (THREE LETTERED PRIMARY SCALES)

اَلصَّرْفُ الصَّغِيْر

The etymologists have created a condensed conjugation to facilitate easy learning of all the detailed conjugation learnt thus far.

1.) فَعَلَ يَفْعُلُ E.g. نَصَرَ يَنْصُرُ He helped.

نَصَرَ يَنْصُرُ نَصْراً فَهُوَ نَاصِرٌ وَنُصِرَ يُنْصَرُ نَصْراً فَهُوَ مَنْصُوْرٌ
الأمر منه: اُنْصُرْ، والنّهى عنهُ: لَاتَنْصُرْ، الظرف منه: مَنْصَرٌ
والآلة منه، مِنْصَرٌ، وأفعل التفضيل المذكر منه: اَنْصَرُ، والمؤنث منه: نُصْرَىٰ

مَصَادِرْ

خَلَق	نَظَر	سُجُوْد	عبادة	دخول
to create	to look	to prostrate	to worship	to enter

Note: The speciality (خَاصِيَة) of this baab is مُغَالَبَه (literally meaning: for one to gain dominance over another in a contest). This speciality only exists when the مُجَرَّدْ verb appears after a verb from بَابُ الْمُفَاعَلَةْ even though that verb originally does not belong to baab نَصَرَ يَنْصُرُ

E.g. يُخَاصِمُنِيْ زَيْدٌ فَأَخْصَمَهُ - Zaid and I are arguing. However, I am overpowering him in arguing.

Note that خَصَمَ comes from baab (ض), however, since مُغَالَبَهْ was intended therefore it was converted to baab (ن)

2.) فَعَلَ يَفْعِلُ E.g. ضَرَبَ يَضْرِبُ He hit.

ضَرَبَ، يَضْرِبُ، ضَرْباً، فهو ضَارِبٌ، وَضُرِبَ، يُضْرَبُ، ضَرْباً، فهو مَضْرُوْبٌ
الأمر منه: اِضْرِبْ، والنهى عنه: لاتَضْرِبْ، الظرف منه : مَضْرِبٌ
والآلة منه: مِضْرَبٌ، وأفعل التفضيل المذكر منه: اَضْرَبُ، والمؤنث منه: ضُرْبَىٰ

مَصَادِرْ

كَسْر	عِرْفَانٌ	غَلَبٌ	فَصْلٌ	جُلُوْس	ظُلْمٌ
to break	to recognize	to overpower	to separate	to sit	to opperess

Note: the speciality of this scale is also مُغَالَبَة on condition that a verb from بَابُ الْمُفَاعَلَة is brought before it (as mentioned earlier).

E.g يُبَايِعُنِيْ زَيْدٌ فَأَبِيْعُهُ - Zaid and I are conducting trade and I have the upper hand in the transaction.

This speciality of ضَرَبَ is generally used with verbs which have a waaw or yaa in the فَا كَلْمَه or yaa in the عَيْن كَلْمَه.

3.) فَعِلَ يَفْعَلُ E.g سَمِعَ يَسْمَعُ He heard

سَمِعَ يَسْمَعُ سَمْعاً، فهو سَامِعٌ، وسُمِعَ يُسْمَعُ سَمْعاً، فهو مَسْمُوْعٌ،
الأمر منه: اِسْمَعْ، والنهى عنه: لاتَسْمَعْ، الظرف منه:مَسْمَعٌ
والآ لة منه: مِسْمَعٌ، و أفعل التفضيل المذكر منه: اَسْمَعُ، والمونث منه: سُمْعٰى

مَصَادِرْ :

شَهَادَةٌ	حَمْدٌ	فَهْمٌ	لَعْبٌ	عِلْمٌ
to bear witness	to praise	to understand	to play	to know

The speciality of this scale is that it is generally intransitive (laazim). It generally gives the following meanings:

i.)	Happiness	E.g.	فَرِحَ بَكْرٌ	Bakr was happy.
ii.)	Sorrow	E.g.	حَزِنَ يُوْسُفُ	Yusuf was sad / grieved.
iii.)	Colours	E.g.	كَدِرَ التُّرَابُ	The sand was muddy coloured.
iv.)	Defects	E.g.	عَوِرَ دَجَّالٌ	Dajjal was one eyed.
v.)	Features of the body	E.g.	بَلِجَ عَبْدُاللهِ	Abdullah had thick eyebrows.
vi.)	Sickness	E.g.	سَقِمَ خَالِدٌ	Khalid was sick.
			مَرِضَ اَبُوْكَ	Your father was sick.

4.) فَعَلَ يَفْعَلُ E.g. فَتَحَ يَفْتَحُ He opened

فَتَحَ ،يَفْتَحُ ،فَتْحاً، فهو فَاتِحٌ، وفُتِحَ ،يُفْتَحُ فَتْحًا، فهو مَفْتُوْحٌ،
الأمرمِنهُ اِفْتَحْ، والنهى عنه:لاتَفْتَحْ، الظرفُ منه: مَفْتَحٌ
والآلة منه: مِفْتَحٌ، وافعل التفضيل المذكر منه: اَفْتَحُ، والمؤنث منه: فُتْحٰى

مَصَادِرْ

صَبَغَ	مَنَعَ	سَلَخَ	رَهَنَ
to dye	to prevent	To peel	to pawn

The speciality of this scale is in its literal construction i.e. The عَيْنَ كَلْمَه or لَامْ كَلْمَه (middle or final radical) are usually amongst those letters which originate from the throat. The six letters which are termed the hurooful halqi are خ غ ح ع ه ء .

Examples:	مَنَعَ مُحَمَّدٌ زَيْدًا	Muhammad prevented Zaid.
	نَهَضَ الطِّفْلُ	The child got up.
	ذَهَبَتْ فَاطِمَةُ	Fatima went.
	سَلَخْتُ الْبَطَاطَةَ	I peeled the potato.
	صَبَغَ اِبْرَاهِيْمُ الثَّوْبَ	Ebrahim dyed the clothes.
	رَهَنْتِ قَلَادَتَكِ	You pawned your necklace.
	جَحَدَ الْكُفَّارُ	The disbelievers rejected / denied.

5.) فَعُلَ يَفْعُلُ E.g كَرُمَ يَكْرُمُ He honoured.

كَرُمَ ،يَكْرُمُ ،كَرْماً، فهوكَرِيْمٌ، الأمرمنه: اُكْرُمْ ، والنهى عنه : لاتَكْرُمْ

الظرف منه:مَكْرَمٌ،وأفعل التفضيل المذكرمنه: اَكْرَمُ ،والمؤنث منه:كُرْمٰى

لَطَافَةٌ	بُعْدٌ	كَثْرَةٌ	صِغَارٌ / صَغَارَةٌ	كُبْرٌ / كِبَارَةٌ	قُرْبٌ
to be gentle; thin; fine	to be far	to be plentful	to be small	to be big; great	to be near

Note: This scale is always laazim (intransitive).

e.g. بَعُدَتْ دِمِشْقُ Damascus was far. كَبُرَ مُحَمَّدٌ Muhammad was great.

It gives the meaning of:

1) Permanent qualities,

E.g. حَسُنَ يُوْسُفُ Yusuf was handsome صَغُرَتِ الْمَرْأَةُ The woman was small (in built).

2.) Temporary qualities which after experience and practice, sort of become permanent,

E.g. فَقُهَ اَبُوْحَنِيْفَة Abu Hanifa had deep understanding.

شَجُعَ الْعَسْكَرِيُّ The soldier was brave.

3.) Natural qualities,

E.g. جَنُبَتِ الثِّيَابُ The clothes were impure. طَهُرَ الْمَاءُ The water was pure.

Note: An intransitive verb (اَلْفِعْلُ اللَّازِم) can be made transitive (مُتَعَدِّى) by inserting the particle after it. E.g. كَرُمَ زَيْدٌ بِعَمْرٍو Zaid was respected by Amr.

The مَجْهُوْل form will now be كُرِمَ بِعَمْرٍو He was respected by Amr.

جَاءَ حَامِدٌ بِكِتَابٍ Haamid brought the book.

جِيْئَ بِكِتَابٍ The book was brought.

6.) فَعِلَ يَفْعِلُ E.g حَسِبَ يَحْسِبُ He thought.

حَسِبَ ،يَحْسِبُ ،حِسْبَانًا فهو حَاسِبٌ،وحُسِبَ ،يُحْسَبُ حِسْبَانًا، فهو مَحْسُوْبٌ الأمر منه:اِحْسِبْ ،والنهى عنه : لاتَحْسِبْ ، الظرف منه: مَحْسِبٌ والآلَةُمنه: مِحْسَبٌ، وأفعل التفضيل المذكرمنه: اَحْسَبُ، والمؤنث منه: حُسْبٰى

مَصَادِرْ

نِعْمَةٌ	to bestow with blessings; to live in luxury; to favour

The speciality of this scale is that it has only two words which are صَحِيْح . They are حَسِبَ and نَعِمَ . Saheeh refers to such a verb which does not contain a harf - ul - illat, a hamza, nor two letters of the same type in the original letters. The remaining words which fall under this baab begin with a waaw or yaa.

E.g. وَلِيَ He came close وَثِقَ He relied وَرِمَ He swelled
يَئِسَ He lost hope يَبِسَ It became dry.

Exercise:

1.) Draw up the sarf - us - sagheer of all the words listed under مَصَادِر

2.) Translate the following words and state which scale they fall on:

a.) رَجَعَ b.) حَصَلَ c.) صَدَقَ d.) رَقَدَ e.) هَزِمَ

f.) رَكِبَ g.) زَرَعَ h.) بَذَلَ i.) قَدَمَ j.) نَفَعَ

LESSON 24

CONDENSED CONJUGATIONS OF THE FOURTEEN ثُلَاثِیْ مَزِیْد فِیْه SCALES (THREE LETTERED DERIVED SCALES)

ثُلَاثِیْ مَزِیْد فِیْه is divided into two groups:

1.) Nine scales contain a هَمْزَةُ الْوَصل .They are:

1 اِفْتِعَال

2 اِسْتِفْعَال

3 اِنْفِعَال

4 اِفْعِلَال

5 اِفْعِيْلَال

6 اِفْعِيْعَال

7 اِفْعِوَّال

8 اِفَّاعُل

9 اِفَّعُّل

2.) Five scales that do not have a هَمْزَةُ الْوَصل . They are:

1 اِفْعال

2 تفعِيْل

3 تَفَعُّل

4 مُفَاعَلَة

5 تَفَاعُل

Special note should be taken of the change in meaning from one form to the other.

1.) اِفْتِعَال E.g. اِجْتِنَاب To refrain

اِجْتَنَبَ ،يَجْتَنِبُ اِجْتِنَاباً، فهو مُجْتَنِبٌ، وَ اُجْتُنِبَ ،يُجْتَنَبُ اِجْتِنَاباً، فهو مُجْتَنَبٌ
الأمر منه:اِجْتَنِبْ ،والنَّهى عنه:لا تَجْتَنِبْ

مَصَادِرْ:

اِقْتِنَاصٌ	اِحْتِمَالٌ	اِعْتِزَالٌ
To hunt	To carry; endure	To isolate oneself

This scale has a number of specialities. It often has the same meaning as the root form (mujarrad)

E.g. حَمَلَ To carry, اِحْتَمَلَ To carry.

It also means to endure suffering.

One speciality of this scale is اِتِّخَاذ i.e to make / do something out of the source (the verbs) or to bring something into the source (verb).

E.g.

اِجْتَحَرَ الْفَارُّ	The mouse made a hole.
اِصْتَنَم اٰزَرْ	Azar made an idol.
اِحْتَجَرَتِ الْمَرْأَةُ الصَّبِيَّ	The woman took the child into her lap.

اِجْتَحَرَ	is made from the word	جَحَرَ
اِصْتَنَمَ	is made from the word	صَنَمَ
اِحْتَجَرَ	is made from the word	حَجَرَ

2.) اِسْتِفْعَالْ E.g. اِسْتِنْصَارْ To seek help.

> اِسْتَنْصَرَ، يَسْتَنْصِرُ، اِسْتِنْصَاراً، فهو مُسْتَنْصِرٌ واُسْتُنْصِرَ يُسْتَنْصَرُ اِسْتِنْصَاراً، فهو مُسْتَنْصَرٌ
>
> الأمر منه: اِسْتَنْصِرْ والنهى عنه: لاتَسْتَنْصِرْ ،لاتُسْتَنْصَرْ

مَصَادِرْ:

اِسْتِفْسَارًا	To ask for elucidation / explanation
اِسْتِغْفَارًا	To seek forgiveness
اِسْتِخْلَافًا	To appoint a successor (lit.: To seek a successor)
اِسْتِمْتَاعًا	To benefit, (lit.: to seek benefit)

One speciality of this scale is طَلَبْ i.e to seek.

E.g.

غَفَرَ	He forgave	اِسْتَغْفَرَ	He sought forgiveness
أَذِنَ	He permitted	اِسْتَأْذَنَ	He sought permission
عَلِمَ	He knew	اِسْتَعْلَمَ	He asked for information

3.) اِنْفِعَال E.g. اِنْفِطَار To split; break apart

اِنْفَطَرَ يَنْفَطِرُ اِنْفِطَاراً، فهو مُنْفَطِرٌ،الأمر منه: اِنْفَطِرْ، والنهى عنه: لاتَنْفَطِرْ

مَصَادِرْ:

اِنْشِعَابًا	اِنْقِلَابًا	اِنْصِرَافًا
To be branched out	To be changed	To be turned

The speciality of this scale is that it is intransitive. It also gives the meaning of succumbing to something.

E.g. اَلْخَدعُ To deceive,

اَلْاِنْخِدَاعُ To allow oneself to be deceived.

4.) اِفْعِلَال E.g. اِحْمِرَار To be red

اِحْمَرَّ يَحْمَرُّ اِحْمِرَاراً، فهو مُحْمَرٌّ،الأمر منه: اِحْمَرِرْ، والنهى عنه: لاتَحْمَرَّ

مَصَادِرْ:

اِخْضِرَارًا	اِصْفِرَارًا	اِبْيِضَاضًا
To be green	To be yellow	To be white

5.) اِفْعِيْلَال E.g. اِدْهِيْمَام To be black

اِدْهَامَّ ،يَدْهَامُّ ،اِدْهِيْمَاماً، فهو مُدْهَامٌّ الأمر منه:اِدْهَامِمْ، والنهى عنه :لاتَدْهَامِمْ

مَصَادِرْ:

اِسْحِيْرَارًا	اِسْمِيْرَارًا	اِكْمِيْتَاتًا
For grass to be very dry	To be very brown	For horses to be suppressed

The above two scales have four specialities each:

1.) لُزُوْم It is intransitive

2.)	مُبَالَغه	Exaggeration
3.)	لَوْن	Colour
4.)	عَيْب	Defect.

E.g.	اِحْمَرَّ الثِّيَابُ	The clothes were very red.
	اِحْوَلَّ الرَّجُلُ	The man was very deaf.
	اِشْهَابَّ اللِّحْيَةُ	The beard was very white.

6.) اِفْعِيْعَال E.g. اِخْشِيْشَان To be very rough

اِخْشَوْشَنَ يَخْشَوْشِنُ اِخْشِيْشَانًا، فهو مُخْشَوْشِنٌ، الأمر منه: اِخْشَوْشِنْ، والنهى عنه: لا تَخْشَوْشِنْ

مَصَادِرْ:

اِخْلِيْلَاقًا	اِخْرِيْرَاقًا	اِمْلِيْلَاحًا
For clothes to be very old	For clothes to be very torn	For water to be salty

The speciality of this scale is:

1.)	لُزُوْم	It is intransitive
2.)	مُبَالَغه	Exaggeration
e.g.	اِعْشَوْشَبَتِ الْأَرْضُ	The earth became very grassy.

7.) اِفْعِوَّال E.g. اِجْلِوَّاذ To run very fast

اِجْلَوَّذَ، يَجْلَوِّذُ،اِجْلِوَّاذاً، فهو مُجْلَوِّذٌ الأمر منه: اِجْلَوِّذْ، والنهى عنه:لا تَجْلَوِّذْ

مَصَادِرْ:

اِخْرِوَّاطًا	اِعْلِوَّاقًا
To peel a stick	To yoke a camel

This scale has no word for ثُلَاثِيْ مُجَرَّدْ . It has been placed directly on the ثُلَاثِيْ مَزِيْد فِيْه scale

8.) اِفَّاعُل E.g. اِثَّاقُل To be heavy

اِثَّاقَلَ ،يَثَّاقَلُ ،اِثَّاقُلاً، فهومُثَّاقِلٌ ،الأمرمنه:اِثَّاقَلْ ، والنهى عنه:لاتَثَّاقَلْ

مَصَادِر:

الْإِدَّارُك	الْإِشَّابُهْ	الْإِصَّالُح
To reach	To resemble	To reconcile

9.) اِفَّعُّل E.g. اِطَّهُّر To be pure

اِطَّهَّرَ ،يَطَّهَّرُ اِطَّهُّرًا، فهو مُطَّهِّرٌ،الأمرمنه:اِطَّهَّرْ، والنهى عنه: لاتَطَّهَّرْ

Scales number eight and nine were originally with a ت . A hamza was added to facilitate easy recitation of the words. The original was تَثَاقَلَ يَتَثَاقَلُ تَثَاقُلاً - تَطَهَّرَ يَتَطَهَّرُ تَطَهُّرًا .

The ت was changed to a ث / ط respectively and then the two ث / ط were incorporated (idghaam). Since a word which begins with a tashdeed cannot be pronounced thus a hamza was placed before it.

Hence: اِثَّاقَلَ - اِطَّهَّرَ

Note : The last four scales are the least used scales of ثُلَاثِيْ مَزِيْد فِيْه .

The five scales which do not contain a هَمْزَةُ الْوَصْل are:

1 اِفْعَال

2 تَفْعِيْل

3 تَفَعُّل

4 مُفَاعَلَة

5 تَفَاعُل

1.) اِفْعَال E.g. اِكْرَام To honour

اَكْرَمَ ،يُكْرِمُ ،اِكْرَاماً، فهومُكْرِمٌ، وَاُكْرِمَ ،يُكْرَمُ ،اِكْرَاماً فهومُكْرَمٌ الأمر منه:اَكْرِمْ ، والنهى عنه: لاتُكْرِمْ

مَصَادِر:

اَلْاِسْلَامُ	اِلْاِعْلَانُ	اَلْاِذْهَابُ	اَلْاِكْمَالُ
To submit	To announce	To take	To complete

The speciality of this scale is تَعْدِيَه - It is the transitive of intransitive verbs, i.e. Those verbs that are لَازِم in مُجَرَّد will become مُتَعَدِّى in بَابُ الْاِفْعَال .

E.g. خَرَجَ زَيْدٌ Zaid came out اَخْرَجْتُهُ I took him out.

If the verb is مُتَعَدِّى with one مَفْعُوْل in mujarrad it will be مُتَعَدِّى with two مَفْعُوْل s in بَابُ الْاِفْعَال .

E.g. حَفَرْتُ نَهْرًا I dug a river اَحْفَرْتُ زَيْدًا نَهْرًا I made Zaid dig a river.

And if it is مُتَعَدِّى with two مَفْعُوْل in mujarrad it will be مُتَعَدِّى with three مَفْعُوْل s in baab if 'aal.

E.g. عَلِمْتُ زَيْدًا فَاضِلًا I knew Zaid to be virtuous

اَعْلَمْتُ زَيْدًا عَمْرًا فَاضِلاً I informed Zaid that Amr is virtuous

Note 1: The hamza in بَابُ الْاِفْعَال is قَطْعِيْ (permanent) not وَصْلِيْ (temporary). The مُضَارِعْ ought to be يُأَكْرِمُ. However, in the وَاحِدْ مُتَكَلِّمْ segha أُأَكْرِمُ there are two hamzas together. One is deleted. Thus in order that all the seghas conform with each other the hamza was dropped off throughout.

Note 2: The اَمْرْ is made from تُأَكْرِمُ and thus becomes اَكْرِمْ .

2.) تَفْعِيْل E.g. تَصْرِيْف To turn

صَرَّفَ، يُصَرِّفُ، تَصْرِيْفاً، فهومُصَرِّفٌ، وصُرِّفَ، يُصَرَّفُ، تَصْرِيْفاً، فهومُصَرَّفٌ،

الأمرمنه: صَرِّفْ والنهى عنه: لاتُصَرِّفْ

مَصَادِر:

تَقْدِيْمٌ	To send forward / be ahead
تَعْجِيْلٌ	To hasten
تَمْكِيْنٌ	To strengthen; to consolidate
تَعْظِيْمٌ	To attach great importance to, to exalt, to honour

The speciality of this scale is تَعْدِيَه . Another speciality is مُبَالَغه It emphasizes the meaning of the verb

E.g. صَرَّحَ الْاَمْرُ The matter became very clear.

3.) تَفَعُّل E.g. تَقَبُّل To accept

تَقَبَّلَ، يَتَقَبَّلُ، تَقَبُّلًا، فهومُتَقَبِّلٌ، وتُقُبِّلَ، يُتَقَبَّلُ، تَقَبُّلاً، فهو مُتَقَبَّلٌ، الأمرمنه: تَقَبَّل والنهى عنه: لاتَتَقَبَّل

مَصَادِرْ:

تَبَسُّمٌ	تَعَجُّلٌ	تَلَبُّسٌ	تَفَكُّهٌ
To smile	To hasten	To hesitate; to stay; to linger	To enjoy

The speciality of this baab is

a.) تَكَلُّف - to pretend.

E.g. تَكَوَّفَ عَمْرٌو Amr pretended to be from Kufa.

تَشَجَّعَ زَيْدٌ Zaid pretended to be brave.

b.) اِتِّخَاذ - to make or take.

E.g. تَبَوَّبَ زَيْدٌ Zaid made a door. تَوَسَّدَ الْحَجَرَ زَيْدٌ Zaid made the stone a pillow.

تَأَبَّطَ الصَّبِيَّ عَمْرٌو Amr took the child in his arms.

4.) مُفَاعَلَه E.g مُقَاتَلَة To fight one another

قَاتَلَ، يُقَاتِلُ، مُقَاتَلَةً، فهو مُقَاتِلٌ، وَقُوْتِلَ، يُقَاتَلُ، مُقَاتَلَةً، فهومُقَاتَلٌ

الأمر منه: قَاتِلْ، والنهى عنه: لاتُقَاتِلْ

مَصَادِرْ:

اَلْمُخَادَعَةُ وَالْخِدَاعُ	اَلْمُعَاقَبَةُ وَالْعِقَابُ	اَلْمُلَازَمَةُ وَاللِّزَامُ	اَلْمُبَارَكَةُ
To deceive each other	To punish one another	To adhere / cling to each other	To bless

The most common speciality of this baab is مُشَارَكَتْ i.e. two people to do a task in such a way that both are the فَاعِلْ and both are the مَفْعُوْل .

E.g. قَاتَلَ زَيْدٌ عَمْرًو Zaid and Amr fought.

From amongst the examples given اَلْمُبَارَكَةُ will not contain this speciality.

5.) تَفَاعُل E.g. تَقَابُل To face one another

تَقَابَلَ ،يَتَقَابَلُ ،تَقَابُلًا، فهومُتَقَابِلٌ، وتُقُوْبِلَ ،يُتَقَابَلُ ،تَقَابُلاً، فهومُتَقَابَلٌ،
الأمرمنه: تَقَابَلْ والنهى عنه: لاتَتَقَابَلْ

مَصَادِر:

اَلتَّفَاخُرُ	اَلتَّعَارُفُ	اَلتَّخَافُتُ
To vie with one another in boasting	To recognize one another	To speak secretly

The most common speciality of this baab is تَشَارُكْ i.e. the action takes place between two people.
E.g. تَلَاطَمَ زَيْدٌ عَمْرًا Zaid and Amr exchanged blows.

The difference between مُشَارَكَتْ and تَشَارُكْ is in إِعْرَابْ only , not in meaning i.e. in مُشَارَكَتْ one party will be given a dhamma and the other a fatha. However, in تَشَارُكْ both parties will have a dhamma.
E.g. عَارَفَ زَيْدٌعَمْرًا - تَعَارَفَ زَيْدٌ عَمْرًا - Zaid and Amr recognized each other.

Note : The mudharie of بَابُ الْإِفْعَال , تَفْعِيْل and مُفَاعَلَه begin with a dhamma.

Exercise:

1.) Write out the sarf - us - sagheer of all the مَصَادِر .

2.) Transform the following words into the fourteen scales. Write out the condensed conjugation of all fourteen scales noting the change in the meaning as the word changes from form to form.

a.) قَتَلَ b.) قَبِلَ

LESSON 25

CONDENSED CONJUGATIONS OF THE رُبَاعِیْ مُجَرَّدْ وَمَزِیْد فِیْه SCALES (FOUR LETTERED PRIMARY AND DERIVED SCALES)

رُبَاعِیْ is made by adding one extra laam to ثُلَاثِیْ. The scale of رُبَاعِیْ is thus: فَعْلَلَ

رُبَاعِیْ مُجَرَّدْ contains only one scale: فَعْلَلَةٌ . Sometimes the masdar فِعْلَالٌ is also used.

e.g. زَلْزَلَ يُزَلْزِلُ زِلْزَالاً

1.) فَعْلَلَةٌ E.g. بَعْثَرَةٌ To scatter

> بَعْثَرَ يُبَعْثِرُ بَعْثَرَةً فَهُوَ مُبَعْثِرٌ،وَبُعْثِرَ يُبَعْثَرُبَعْثَرَةً فَهُوَ مُبَعْثَرٌ
>
> الأمر منه: بَعْثِرْ، والنهى عنه:لَاتُبَعْثِرْ

مَصَادِرْ:

قَنْطَرَةٌ	زَعْفَرَةٌ	عَسْكَرَةٌ	دَحْرَجَةٌ
To build a bridge	To dye with saffron	To prepare an army	To roll

The مُضَارِعْ of the above scale begins with a dhamma.

رُبَاعِیْ مَزِیْد فِیْه is divided into two types:

1.) Two scales have a هَمْزَةُ الْوَصْلِ . (They are both intransitive.)

1.) اِفْعِنْلَالٌ E.g. اِبْرِنْشَاقٌ To be happy

> اِبْرَنْشَقَ يَبْرَنْشِقُ اِبْرِنْشَاقًا فَهُوَ مُبْرَنْشِقٌ، اَلاَمْرُمِنْهُ:اِبْرَنْشِقْ ، وَالنَّهْىُ عنه:لاتَبْرَنْشِقْ

مَصَادِرْ:

اِحْرِنْجَامًا	اِعْرِنْكَاسًا	اِسْلِنْطَاحًا
To gather	For hair to be black	To sleep on a pillow

2.) اِفْعِلَّالٌ E.g. اِقْشِعْرَارٌ To shiver / hair to stand on end

> اِقْشَعَرَّ يَقْشَعِرُّ اِقْشِعْرَاراً،فهومُقْشَعِرٌّ،الأمر منه: اِقْشَعِرَّ اِقْشَعِرِّاقْشَعْرِرْ،
>
> والنهى عنه : لاتَقْشَعِرَّ لاتَقْشَعِرِّ لاتَقْشَعْرِرْ،

مَصَادِرْ:

اَلْاِقْمِطْرَار	اَلْاِشْفِتْرَار	اَلْاِزْمِهْرَار
To be very unhappy	To pout	For eyes to red

One scale has a هَمْزَةُ الْوَصْل (this scale is also intransitive).

1.) تَفَعْلَلَ E.g. تَسَرْبَلَ To wear clothes

تَسَرْبَلَ يَتَسَرْبَلُ تَسَرْبُلاً فَهُوَ مُتَسَرْبِلٌ،الاَمْرمنه:تَسَرْبَلْ،والنهى عنه:لاتَسَرْبَلْ

مَصَادِرْ:

اَلتَّبَخْتُرُ	اَلتَّقَهْقُرُ	اَلتَّبَرْقُعُ
To walk with pride; to strut	To be retreat , to deteriorate	To wear a burqa

Note 1: Each scale has many specialities. All of them have not been mentioned.

Note 2: The following eleven scales are always intransitive:

1.	كَرُمَ	7.	اِفَّعُّل
2.	اِنْفِعَال	8.	اِفَّاعُل
3.	اِفْعِلَال	9.	اِفْعِنْلَالٌ
4.	اِفْعِيْلَال	10.	اِفْعِلَّالٌ
5.	اِفْعِيْعَال	11.	تَفَعْلُلٌ
6.	اِفْعِوَّال		

Note 3: They can be made مُتَعَدِّیْ by adding an appropriate حَرْفُ الْجَارْ (Harf - ul - jar) after it. Generally the particle ب is used.

E.g. اُصْفُرَّ بِالزَّعْفَرَانِ - It was made yellow with saffron.

Note 4: Four scales begin with a dhamma in مُضَارِعْ but this does not denote passivity. They are:

1	اِفْعَال	2	تَفْعِيْل	3	مُفَاعَلَه	4	تَفَاعُلْ

A COMPREHENSIVE DIAGRAM OF THE DIVISION OF VERBS

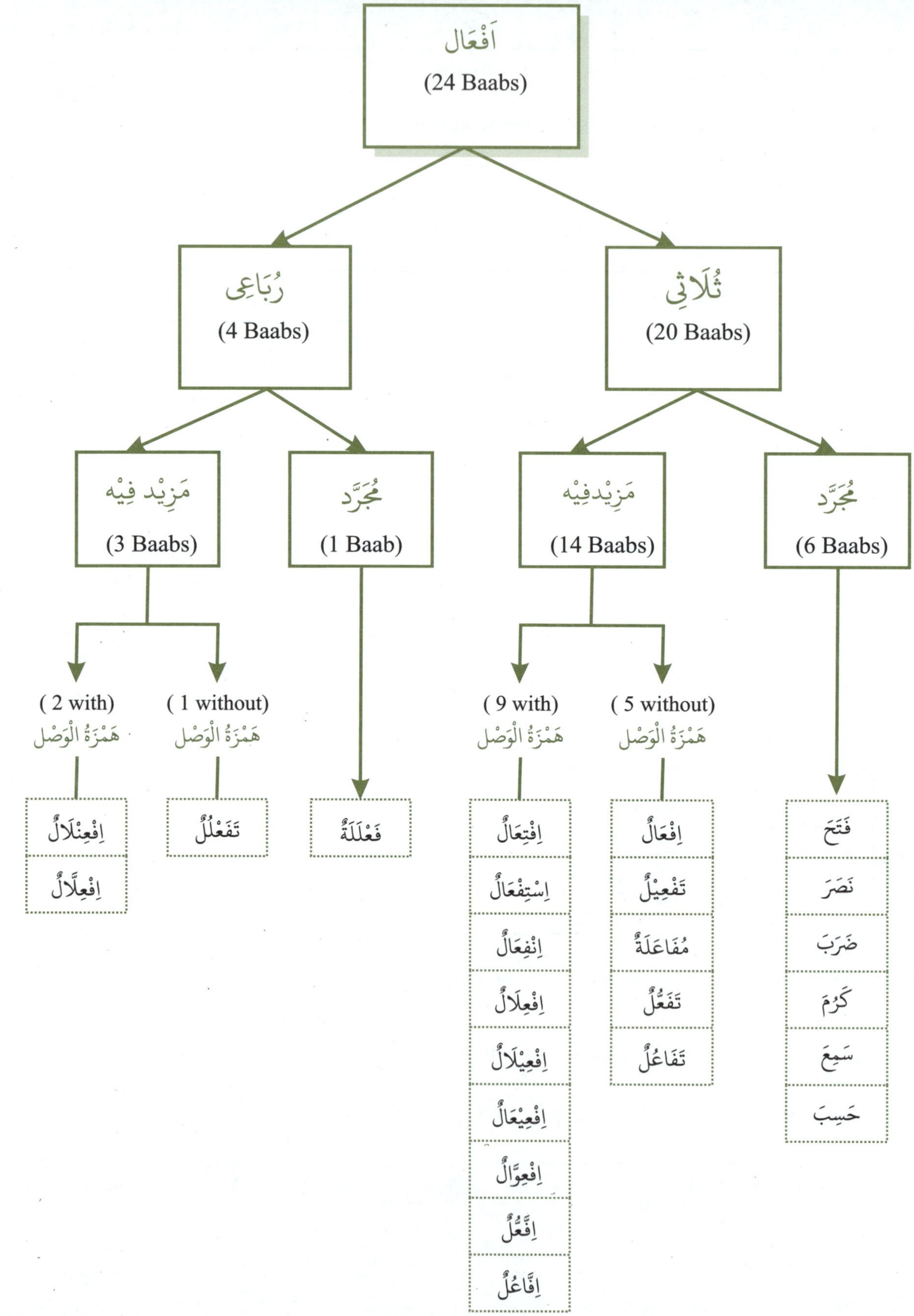

Exercise:

1.) Translate the following.

2.) Identify the verbs and derivative nouns in each sentence and aayat and state which baab each word comes from.

3.) Write down the بحث and segha of each word.

لَطِیْفَه

قَالَ لَا تَخَفْ فَإِنَّهُ يُسَبِّحُ قَالَ إِنِّیْ اَخَافُ اَنْ تُدْرِكَهُ الرِّقَّةُ فَيَسْجُدُ

قَالَ مُسْتَأْجِرٌ لِصَاحِبِ الْبَيْتِ اَصْلِحْ خَشَبَ هٰذَا السَّقْفِ فَإِنَّهُ يُفَرْقِعُ

And from the Qur'aan:

١) ﴿ وَاجْتَنِبُوْا قَوْلَ الزُّوْرِ ﴾(سورة الحج: ٣٠)

٢) ﴿ حَافِظُوْا عَلَى الصَّلَوٰتِ وَالصَّلَاةِ الْوُسْطٰى ﴾ (سورة البقرة: ٢٣٨)

٣) ﴿ وَاسْتَغْفِرُوْا اللهَ إِنَّ اللهَ غَفُوْرٌ رَّحِيْمٌ ﴾(سورة المزمّل: ٢٠)

٤) ﴿ يَا اَيُّهَا الرَّسُوْلُ بَلِّغْ مَا أُنْزِلَ إِلَيْكَ مِنْ رَّبِّكَ ﴾ (سورة المائدة: ٦٧)

٥) ﴿ وَذَكِّرْ فَإِنَّ الذِّكْرٰى تَنْفَعُ الْمُؤْمِنِيْنَ ﴾ (سورة الذاريات: ٥٥)

٦) ﴿ إِنَّ الْمُبَذِّرِيْنَ كَانُوْا إِخْوَانَ الشَّيَاطِيْنِ ﴾ (سورة الإسراء: ٢٧)

٧) ﴿ وَنَزَّلْنَا مِنَ السَّمَاءِ مَاءً مُّبَارَكًا فَاَنْبَتْنَا بِهِ جَنّٰتٍ وَّحَبَّ الْحَصِيْدِ ﴾ (سورة ق: ٩)

٨) ﴿ إِذْ قَالَ لَهُ رَبُّهُ اَسْلِمْ قَالَ اَسْلَمْتُ لِرَبِّ الْعَالَمِيْنَ ﴾ (سورة البقرة: ١٣١)

٩) ﴿ يَوْمَ تَبْيَضُّ وُجُوْهٌ وَّتَسْوَدُّ وُجُوْهٌ فَاَمَّا الَّذِيْنَ ابْيَضَّتْ وُجُوْهُهُمْ فَفِيْ رَحْمَةِ اللهِ ﴾ (سورة آل عمران: ١٠٦)

١٠) ﴿ إِنَّ اللهَ لَا يُخْلِفُ الْمِيْعَادَ ﴾ (سورة آل عمران: ٩)

١١) ﴿ اَفَلَا يَعْلَمُ إِذَا بُعْثِرَ مَا فِي الْقُبُوْرِ ﴾ (سورة العاريات: ٩)

١٢) ﴿ اَلَا بِذِكْرِ اللهِ تَطْمَئِنُّ الْقُلُوْبُ ﴾(سورة الرعد: ٢٨)

١٣) ﴿ فَمَنْ زُحْزِحَ عَنِ النَّارِ وَاُدْخِلَ الْجَنَّةَ فَقَدْ فَازَ ﴾ (سورة آل عمران: ١٨٥)

١٤) ﴿ هٰذَا مُغْتَسَلٌ بَارِدٌ وَّشَرَابٌ ﴾(سورة ص: ٤٢)

VOCABULARY
THERE LETTERED VERBS

TRANSLATION	WORD	TRANSLATION	WORD
He did.	فَعَلَ	He overpowered.	غَلَبَ
He hit.	ضَرَبَ	He cleaned.	نَظَفَ
He wrote.	كَتَبَ	He came close.	قَرُبَ
He heard.	سَمِعَ	It was little.	قَلَّ
He knew.	عَلِمَ	He cooked.	طَبَخَ
He hepled.	نَصَرَ	He sat.	قَعَدَ
He killed.	قَتَلَ	He learnt.	دَرَسَ
He left.	تَرَكَ	He owned.	مَلَكَ
He opened.	فَتَحَ	He reached.	بَلَغَ
He sat.	جَلَسَ	He understood.	فَهِمَ
He ate.	اَكَلَ	He wounded.	جَرَحَ
He drank.	شَرِبَ	He sank.	خَسَفَ
He laughed.	ضَحِكَ	He was big / great.	كَبُرَ
He prevented / stopped.	مَنَعَ	He favoured.	نَعِمَ
He washed.	غَسَلَ	He gave.	مَنَحَ
He asked.	سَاَلَ	He created.	خَلَقَ
He worshipped.	عَبَدَ	He recognised.	عَرَفَ
He went.	ذَهَبَ	He broke.	كَسَرَ
He prostrated.	سَجَدَ	He witnessed.	شَهِدَ
He called.	دَعَى	He praised.	حَمِدَ
He threw.	رَمَى	He pawned.	رَهَنَ
He oppressed.	ظَلَمَ	He peeled.	سَلَخَ
He bowed down.	رَكَعَ	He dyed.	صَبَغَ
He imprisoned.	سَجَنَ	He was kind / delicate.	لَطُفَ
He entered.	دَخَلَ	It was abundant.	كَثُرَ

TRANSLATION	WORD	TRANSLATION	WORD
He separated.	فَصَلَ	He was small.	صَغُرَ
He took.	اَخَذَ	He came close.	وَلِيَ
He commanded.	اَمَرَ	He swelled.	وَرِمَ
He played.	لَعِبَ	He relied.	وَثِقَ
He sought.	طَلَبَ	He lost hope.	يَئِسَ
He read.	قَرَءَ	He returned.	رَجَعَ
He looked.	نَظَرَ	He reached / attained.	حَصَلَ
He slept.	رَقَدَ	He was truthful	صَدَقَ
He rode.	رَكِبَ	He defeated.	هَزَمَ
He spent.	بَذَلَ	He planted.	زَرَعَ
He benefited.	نَفَعَ	He came forward.	قَدَمَ
He made an excuse.	عَذَرَ	He gave permission.	سَمَحَ

WORDS WITH MORE THAN THREE LETTERS

TRANSLATION	WORD	TRANSLATION	WORD
He refrained.	اِجْتَنَبَ	He carried.	اِحْتَمَلَ
He honoured.	اَكْرَمَ	He submitted.	اَسْلَمَ
He smiled.	تَبَسَّمَ	He deceived.	خَادَعَ
He scattered.	بَعْثَرَ	He rolled.	دَحْرَجَ
He translated.	تَرْجَمَ	He sought forgiveness.	اِسْتَغْفَرَ
It shook.	زَلْزَلَ	He turned.	صَرَّفَ

MASDARS

TRANSLATION	WORD	TRANSLATION	WORD
to be cracked	اِنْفِطَارًا	to wear a burqa	تَبَرْقُعًا
to wear	تَسَرْبُلاً	to be evident	حَصْحَصَةٌ
to gather	اِحْرِنْجَامًا	to prepare an army	عَسْكَرَةٌ

TRANSLATION	WORD	TRANSLATION	WORD
to isolate / separate oneself	اِعْتِزَالًا	to appoint a successor	اِسْتِخْلَافًا
to seek benefit	اِسْتِمْتَاعًا	to be changed	اِنْقِلَابًا
to ask	اِسْتِفْسَارًا	to be turned	اِنْصِرَافًا
to branch out	اِنْشِعَابًا	to be very yellow	اِصْفِرَارًا
to be very red	اِحْمِرَارًا	to be very white	اِبْيِضَاضًا
to be very green	اِخْضِرَارًا	to be very black	اِدْهِيْمَامًا
for horses to be suppressed	اِكْمِيْتَاتًا	to be fawn coloured	اِسْمِيْرَاراً
for grass to be dry	اِصْحِيْرَارً	to be rough	اِخْشِيْشَانًا
for cloths to be old	اِخْلِيْلَاقًا	for clothes to be torn	اِخْرِيْرَاقًا
for water to be salty	اِمْلِيْلَاحًا	for a stick to be peeled	اِخْرِوَّاطًا
to run very fast	اِجْلِوَّاذًا	to be heavy	اِثَّاقُلاً
for a camel to be yoked	اِعْلِوَّاطًا	to be similar / resemble	اِشَّابُهًا
to be reached	اِدَّارُكًا	to be helpess	اِضَّرُّعًا
to reconcile / arbitrate	اِصَّالُحًا	to be covered in a blanket	اِزَّمُّلاً
to accept advice	اِذَّكُّراً	to submit	اِسْلَامًا
to honour	اِكْرَامًا	to complete	اِكْمَالاً
to take	اِذْهَابًا	to turn	تَصْرِيْفًا
to announce	اِعْلَانًا	to hasten	تَعْجِيْلاً
To send forward / be ahead	تَقْدِيْمًا	to attach great importance to	تَعْظِيْمًا
to make place	تَمْكِيْنًا	to smile	تَبَسُّمًا
to accept	تَقَبُّلًا	to deceive	مُخَادَعَةً
to delay	تَلَبُّثًا	to attain blessings	مُبَارَكَةً
to fight	مُقَاتَلَةً	to face each other	تَقَابُلاً
to punish	مُعَاقَبَةً	to scatter	بَعْثَرَةً
to make compulsory on each other	مُلَازَمَةً	to recognize one another	تَعَارُفًا
to vie in boasting	تَفَاخُرًا	to build a bridge	قَنْطَرَةً
to speak secretly to each other	تَخَافُتًا	to shiver / for hair to stand on end	اِقْشِعْرَارًا

TRANSLATION	WORD	TRANSLATION	WORD
to roll	دَحْرَجَةً	to pout	اِشْفِتْرَارًا
for eyes to be red	اِزْمِهْرَارًا	to wear clothes	تَسَرْبُلاً
to be happy	اِبْرِنْشَاقًا	for hair to be black	اِعْرِنْكَاسًا
to sleep on a pillow	اِسْلِنْطَاءً	to shrink / to be very unhappy	اِقْمِطْرَاراً
to colour with saffron	زَعْفَرَةً	to walk with pride / strut	تَبَخْتُرًا

GLOSSARY OF TECHNICAL TERMS

1)	Sarf is the study of that branch of Arabic grammar which deals with the formation, recognition and changing of words from one form to another. It also deals with the correct sequence of the Arabic conjugation (gardaan). Benefit: A person learns to read words correctly.	
2.)	اَلْبَحْث	- Subject under discussion.
3.)	اَلْمُثْبِتْ / اَلْاِثْبَات	- positive, for an action to occur e.g. I ate as opposed to I did NOT eat.
4.)	اَلْفِعْلُ الْمَاضِىْ	- past tense verb e.g. The boy kicked the ball (in the past).
5.)	اَلْمَعْرُوْف	- active, where the doer is known e.g. Zaid hit Amr. One is aware of who did the action of hitting.
6.)	گَرْدَان	- (paradigm / conjugation / inflection) An Urdu term indicating the process or practice of rendering the various forms of the word in its correct order.
7.)	اَلصِّيْغَه	- (mood or form) the explanation of a verb or noun, i.e. a form or forms of a verb indicating fact, tense, command, number etc.
8.)	وَاحِدْ	- singular e.g. One boy
9.)	تَثْنِيَه	- dual e.g. Two boys
10.)	جَمَعْ	- plural e.g. 3 boys , 8 boys
11.)	مُؤَنَّث	- masculine
12.)	مُذَكَّرْ	- feminine
13.)	غَائِبْ	- the third person i.e. A person who is absent e.g. فَعَلَ He did.
14.)	حَاضِرْ	- addressee or the second person. The person who is refered to as "you" e.g. فَعَلْتَ You did.
15.)	مُتَكَلِّمْ	- the speaker who is generally refered to as the first person, It is used when talking of oneself. e.g. فَعَلْتُ "I did" فَعَلْنَا"We did"
16.)	مَنْفِيْ / نَفِيْ	- The negative where an action does not take place e.g. مَا ضَرَبَ He did not hit i.e. the action of hitting did not take place. مَا نَصَرَ He did not help.
17.)	مَجْهُوْل	- a passive verb where the doer is unknown e.g. فُعِلَ He / It was done upon قُتِلَ He was killed. The action of killing took place on him and we do not know who did the action of killing.
18.)	اَلْحُرُوْفُ الْاَصْلِيَّة	- the original or root letters. This refers to all those letters which appear / fall on the scale of ف ، ع and ل .
19.)	اَلْحُرُوْفُ الزَّائِدَة	- (extra letters) all the letters besides those that fall on the scale of ف ، ع and ل are regarded as extra letters or اَلْحُرُوْفُ الزَّائِدَة.
20.)	حَرْكَتْ	- kasra, dhamma, fatha (ُ ِ َ)
21.)	مُضَارِعْ	- refers to a present or future tense verb.

		E.g. يَضْرِبُ He is hitting or will hit يَفْتَحُ He is opening or will open.
22.)	مَفْتُوْحٌ	- A word ending with a fatha
23.)	مَكْسُوْرٌ	- A word ending with a kasra.
24.)	A baab (group / category) is formed when the وَاحِدْ مُذَكَّرْ غَائِبْ of مَاضِىْ and the وَاحِدْ مُذَكَّرْ غَائِبْ of مُضَارِعْ are put together and read. As far as verbs are concerned there are twenty four categories.	
25.)	اَلْفِعْلُ اللَّازِمْ	(Intransitive verbs) - this refers to such a verb which does not require a to be complete. The sentence is complete with a فَاعِلْ alone, e.g. فَرِحَ زَيْدٌ Zaid was happy. سَكَتَ حَامِدٌ Haamid was silent, جَاءَ الْقَوْمُ The nation / people came.
26.)	اَلْفِعْلُ الْمُتَعَدِّىْ	(Transitive verb) - this refers to a verb which requires a مَفْعُوْل to be complete. e.g. اَكَلَ زَيْدٌ الْخُبْزَ Zaid ate the bread. قَتَلَ دَاوُدُ جَالُوْتَ Dawood killed Jaloot.
27.)	تَاكِيْد	- stress or emphasis.
28.)	مُسْتَقْبِلْ	- future tense verb - e.g. He will ask (in future).
29.)	مَنْفِى	- negative, for an action not to occur. e.g. مَا اَكَلْتُ - I did not eat
30.)	اَمْرْ	- is such a word by which a command is given e.g. اِضْرِبْ Hit!, اِرْكَبْ Ride!
31.)	هَمْزَةُ الْوَصْلِ	- is a temporary hamza. It is written but not read when joined to another word, e.g. وَقَالَ ارْكَبُوْا However, when found at the beginning of a statement it will be articulated, e.g. اِرْكَبْ
32.)	نَهِى	- refers to a command which is negative, e.g. لَاتَسْمَعْ Do not listen! لَاتَلْعَبْ Do not play!
33.)	"ن" تاكيد	The emphatic noon (ن تاكيد) is of two types: نْ - "ن" خفيه نّ - "ن" ثقيله

34.)	اِسْمُ الْفَاعِل	- is the noun which explains the doer of the action. It is an ism derived from a مَصْدَرْ (root word) and has a particular scale. In this aspect it differs from a فَاعِل which does not have to be derivative noun. The فَاعِل must be with its فِعْل while an اِسْمُ الْفَاعِل does not need to accompany a فِعْل or فَاعِل . e.g. قَاتِلٌ One male killer. ضَارِبٌ One male who hits.
35.)	اِسْمُ الْمَفْعُوْل	is that noun which explains the person on whom the action is done. It is an اِسْمُ الْمُشْتَق i.e. a noun derived from a مَصْدَر , e.g. قَتَلَ زَيْدٌ اَسَدًا Zaid killed the lion. قَاتِلٌ is the killer i.e. Zaid, مَقْتُوْلٌ is the killed i.e the lion.
36.)	اَلصِفَةُ الْمُشَبَّهَة	is that noun which indicates a permanent quality. It is made from an intransitive verb. e.g. جَمِيْلٌ That person who is permanently beautiful.
37.)	اِسْمُ الْمُبَالَغَه	- is that مَصْدَرْ (derivative) which emphasizes an action itself. It shows intensity in meaning. e.g. ضَرَّابٌ One who hits excessively.
38.)	اِسْمُ التَّفْضِيْل	- is that noun which compares two things. It gives the meaning of better than / greater than. e.g. اَللّٰهُ اَكْبَرُ Allah is not merely great but He is greater than everything else.
39.)	The difference between اِسْمُ التَّفْضِيْل (Elative) and اِسْمُ الْمُبَالَغَه (superlative) is that اِسْمُ الْمُبَالَغَه emphasizes something in itself however, اِسْمُ التَّفْضِيْل compares the greatness between two things. e.g. زَيْدٌ ضَرَّابٌ Zaid hits a lot. زَيْدٌ اَضْرَبُ مِنْ عَمْرٍو Zaid hits more than Amr.	
40.)	اِسْمُ الظَّرْف	is that noun which gives us an idea of the time or place when or where an action occurs.
41.)	ظَرْفُ الْمَكَان	- refers to the place where an action occurse e.g. مَلْعَبٌ - One place of playing.
42.)	ظَرْفُ الزَّمَان	- refers to the time when an action occurs. e.g. مَقْعَدٌ - One time of sitting.
43.)	اِسْمُ الْآلَة	is that noun which names the tool or instrument with which some work is done. e.g. مِضْرَبٌ Instrument of hitting.
44.)	ثُلَاثِي	- A triliteral verb i.e. a verb with three letters. e.g. فَهِمَ - He understood سَجَنَ - He imprisoned

45.)	رُبَاعِى	- A quadriliteral verb i.e. a verb with four letters. e.g. زَلْزَلَ - He shook, he caused to tremble بَعْثَرَ - He scattered.
46.)	مُجَرَّدْ	(The primary / stripped form) - A word which consists of original letters only. It contains no extra letters. e.g. جَرَحَ - He wounded - contains three original letters.
47.)	مَزِيْد فِيْه	(The increased form) - refers to such a word which contains original letters as well as extra letters. e.g. اَسْلَمَ - He submitted - it contains three original letters i.e. سَلَمَ and has one extra letter i.e. Alif
48.)	مَصْدَرْ	- is that word from which nouns and verbs are derived. It gives the meaning of 'to' or 'ing' when translated into English. e.g. ضَرْبٌ To hit or hitting.

Pages 280

Pages 368

Pages 224

Pages 104

Pages 114

Pages 256